PRINCE PHILIP
A Family Portrait

Also by Alexandra—Queen of Yugoslavia

FOR LOVE OF A KING

Portrait of Prince Philip by Pietro Annigoni

Prince Philip

A FAMILY PORTRAIT

by

Alexandra

Queen of Yugoslavia

THE **BOBBS-MERRILL** COMPANY, INC.
A SUBSIDIARY OF HOWARD W. SAMS & CO., INC.
Publishers · INDIANAPOLIS · NEW YORK

For My Dearest Aunt Alice
(*H.R.H. Princess Andrew of Greece*),
Mother of H.R.H. Prince Philip

PRINCE PHILIP
A Family Portrait

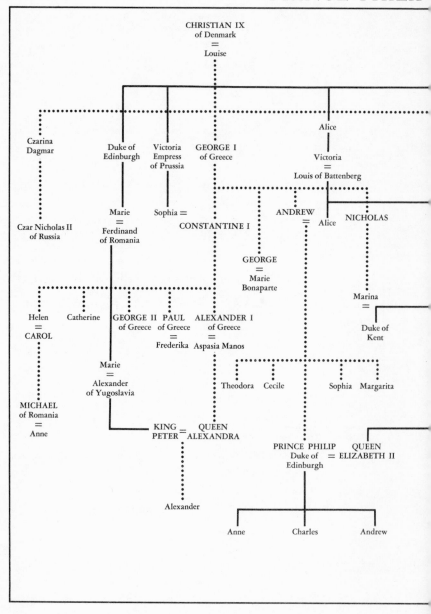

CHRISTIAN IX
of Denmark
=
Louise

Czarina
Dagmar

Duke of
Edinburgh

Victoria
Empress
of Prussia

GEORGE I
of Greece

Alice

Victoria
=
Louis of Battenberg

Czar Nicholas II
of Russia

Marie
=
Ferdinand
of Romania

Sophia =
CONSTANTINE I

ANDREW
=
Alice

NICHOLAS

GEORGE
=
Marie
Bonaparte

Helen
=
CAROL

Catherine

GEORGE II
of Greece

PAUL
of Greece
=
Frederika

ALEXANDER I
of Greece
=
Aspasia Manos

Marina
=
Duke of
Kent

MICHAEL
of Romania
=
Anne

Marie
=
Alexander
of Yugoslavia

Theodora

Cecile

Sophia

Margarita

KING
PETER

=

QUEEN
ALEXANDRA

PRINCE PHILIP
Duke of
Edinburgh

=

QUEEN
ELIZABETH II

Alexander

Anne

Charles

Andrew

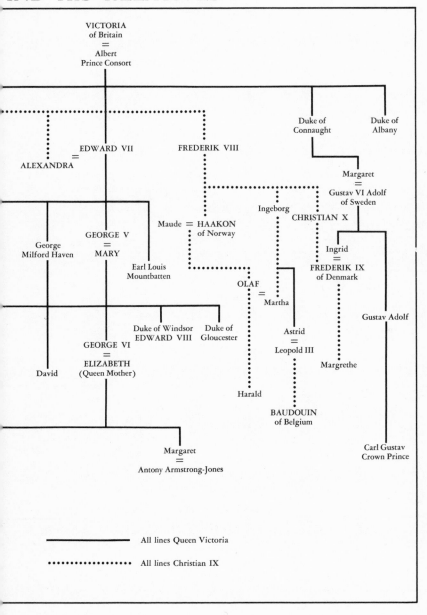

VICTORIA
of Britain
=
Albert
Prince Consort

Duke of
Connaught

Duke of
Albany

EDWARD VII

FREDERIK VIII

ALEXANDRA
=

Margaret
=
Gustav VI Adolf
of Sweden

Ingeborg

CHRISTIAN X

George
Milford Haven

GEORGE V
=
MARY

Maude = HAAKON
of Norway

Ingrid
=
FREDERIK IX
of Denmark

Earl Louis
Mountbatten

OLAF
=
Martha

Gustav Adolf

Duke of Windsor   Duke of
EDWARD VIII   Gloucester

GEORGE VI
=

Astrid
=
Leopold III

David

ELIZABETH
(Queen Mother)

Margrethe

Harald

Margaret
=
Antony Armstrong-Jones

BAUDOUIN
of Belgium

Carl Gustav
Crown Prince

——————— All lines Queen Victoria

•••••••••••••••• All lines Christian IX

Contents

Chapter 1

◆ Alice and Andrea

1

I<small>F</small> I <small>HAD</small> been born a boy, I would have been named His Royal Highness Prince Philip of Greece. My young father, H.M. King Alexander I, had chosen this name and title for me only a month before he died. But I was born instead a Royal Princess. And later, just eleven weeks afterward my Great-aunt Alice and Great-uncle Andrea—T.R.H. Prince and Princess Andrew of Greece—gave the name "Philip" to a new son, in affectionate token to my father's memory.

To a large degree we, Philip and I, have the same long lineage. We are both great-great-grandchildren of H.M. Queen Victoria. We are also both descended from that William George of Schleswig-Holstein-Sonderburg-Glucksberg-Beck, Prince of Denmark, who ascended the throne of Greece as King George I. Both of us owe our breath to the very same loves of long ago.

There is this difference: though we are the same age, Philip belongs to a generation earlier than mine. H.M. King Constantine of Greece was my grandfather, but he was Philip's uncle, the brother of Andrea.

Philip and I swam together as babies in the sunlight of Greece and we cried together in our carriages. Indeed, we shared the same carriage, for our nannies found this the easiest way to divide their job and enjoy their walks.

Philip's father and my father had been the greatest of friends. Perhaps their association was the starting point for a pattern of circumstances that Philip and I have since come to share—first exile and loneliness, then many strange journeys and finally happy alliance in marriage with other royal houses.

In my teens, there was a prospect that I might marry Philip. It was discussed, I know. And though it was decided that we were too closely related, a youthful affection still remains, obscured at times, yet strong.

Perhaps that closeness is why it is so fascinating for me to trace the meteoric progress of my cousin in his challenging, chosen path.

No doubt it is the reason others have so eagerly asked me to write this book. Yet the task is exciting for still another reason. Surely no man in the modern world has so thoroughly fulfilled every potential gift and trait of his personality as Philip has. Surely it is hard to find another public figure who is a more representative man of our age—or a man whose life has had more interesting contrasts.

There is the cousin who patiently used to remind me that he did not spell his name "Philipe" or "Felipe." And there is the consort whom my relatives sometimes call "Philip in his glory."

He was once a refugee baby in an orange crate, yet he married the heiress of the world's greatest realm—his position now regulated by the stately warrant, "Henceforth upon all occasions to have, hold and enjoy Place, Pre-Eminence and Precedence next to Her Majesty . . ."

He has been driven through London in the ancient Coronation coach, and he has lumbered across a German plain hunched at the wheel of the newest-pattern tank.

He has sipped cocoa from a thick mug on a midnight destroyer patrol in the North Sea, and today his health is drunk in champagne around the world.

He delves into nuclear physics and unexpectedly organizes conferences of industrialists and trade union chiefs at Buckingham Palace.

When he wakes up in his paneled bedroom, the husband and helpmeet of a Queen Regnant, does he remember his preposterous youthful romance in Venice—or the nights when, with a boy's love of adventure, he slumbered on sacks of grain in the hold of a Thames sailing barge?

He does know the world as few other men know it, from the sidewalks of New York to the Antarctic solitudes. He has shot crocodiles in the remote northern territories of Australia and placid wild fowl amid the reeds of Eastern England. He has walked at the head of the stately procession of the Order of the Garter, and slaved half-naked in the stokehold of a troopship.

He knows what it is to eat fish and chips in seaport cafés and also what it is to be repeatedly applauded as guest of honor at a banquet in London's Guildhall.

I reflect with pride that my husband, King Peter, gained the palm for *savoir-faire* when he blandly addressed the Houses of Congress from mere headline notes, though only a boy of eighteen. But perhaps Philip equaled this feat in his famous presidential address to the British Association for the Advancement of Science when, with *expertise,* he coolly lectured the assembled scientists for over an hour about the century of achievement Darwin to nuclear fission. The academic applause lasted three whole minutes, a notable triumph . . . and one of so many.

Long ago, when we would walk near the golf course at Phaleron, Philip used to take a stick and trace on the path the plans of a home he dreamed of building one day, after he had made his way in the Navy and had some money to spare.

Now, far from those visionary houses in the sand, he refurbishes and remodels castles and palaces, and indeed continually seeks to renew and reinvigorate an empire.

2

Philip's mother, Princess Alice of Greece, will always appear to me in her severe gray gowns, a nunlike coif at her brow. She was a deaf-mute, and I can never forget her brown eyes fixed unwaveringly on my lips as she lip-read my gossip and girlish talk.

I loved my Aunt Alice deeply. Perhaps I was drawn to her, in my teens, by the sympathy and understanding she displayed for my absurd little problems. Though she was, in fact, my great-aunt, tall and elderly, she seemed one of the rare adults willing to give full attention to a child. She memorized the names of my friends so she could ask about them afterward; she could recall trivial incidents I told her about, with bubbling laughter.

I knew that Alice had been born deaf but I did not understand at first that she had to fight in childhood a crippling handicap in learning how to speak. Because she could not hear, she was slow to realize that words had sounds, and she had difficulty in forming them.

Speech training was then practically in its infancy and only her own marvelous determination gradually mastered the obstacles.

There are still times when Alice plays with words like a child with a new toy, ejaculating them like silver balls in a fountain. At these times she talks for hours as if in triumph, chatting in her deep, throaty way, of friends and events and bygone family history.

I always knew Alice was profoundly religious yet she never said anything to me of religion. I always knew she had been married for more than twenty or thirty years and had her four daughters, all older than I, and a son, yet she never spoke of her husband, my Uncle Andrea.

And looking back, I cannot remember that Aunt Alice has ever talked of herself, though she has led an exciting life indeed.

It was not till years after my teen-age conversations that I learned she had been an eight-year-old bridesmaid at the wedding of my Aunt May and the Duke of York, who later became Queen Mary and King George V.

Or that at the time of the Allied bombardment of Athens in 1916 she drove home through a pitched battle in the streets to find that bullets had shattered the nursery window, scattering glass around her two youngest children, Cecile and Sophie, as they played on the floor.

When my father was called to the throne and my young mother and he were in tears at the responsibility that had so suddenly been placed upon him, it was Alice who first came into the room to put her arms around Mummie and comfort her.

There was family history I witnessed personally.

I remember, when I was eighteen, visiting Aunt Alice in her little house near Kolonaki Square and her continually glancing at the clock at the time when her son Philip was expected. Her deaf lady-in-waiting, Madame Socopol, would come running in with warning gestures whenever a car turned into the street.

To welcome young Philip on these infrequent occasions a large meal was always prepared. One day, it included a compote of whole stewed oranges, unpeeled, which had first been boiled for hours. I must have made a face at the bitter-sweet taste, but Philip liked it, so I politely tried to show appreciation. Thereafter, Aunt Alice often greeted me with the cry, "Sandra, we are having your favorite dessert—orange compote!" and, unable to tell her my true feelings, I had to eat it almost to the point of feeling sick.

On the other hand, Aunt Alice knew that I disliked sauces and attentively had her cook prepare plain food for me, usually something grilled.

But lunch or no lunch, two or three times a week, when in Athens, I would push open the iron gate and have the attendant royal policeman set the doorbell jangling. Then, as in a familiar nest, I would find myself in the overcrowded rooms, crammed with old-fashioned furniture and stocked with signed photographs of innumerable Battenbergs.

Even in England, Aunt Alice rarely abandoned the religious costume she wore for many years. Long before she founded her own nursing order on the isle of Tinos, she experimented with suitably austere clothes, oblivious to any quiet amusement she caused.

When the German invasion of Greece was imminent in 1941, I remember she opened a cupboard door and gave me all her crested notepaper, stamped with an "A" and a crown, because my initial was the same as hers. In its huge Asprey box nearly a yard long, this impractical parting gift had to be stowed aboard a destroyer for evacuation. All or most of our worldly goods were jettisoned overboard when the destroyer was involved in battle action, but the heavy box of notepaper remained, and I used it to the last scrap.

Not that Aunt Alice wasn't aware she could be humorous. At one time she loved to go to a cinema house that showed old silent films, chiefly for the joy of lip-reading what the characters really said. With her infallible memory she would then dramatize these conversations for her friends.

At a dinner party she once described one of the big scenes in, I think, Von Stroheim's "Greed." In the midst of a passionate love scene, the hero was in fact telling the heroine that he was being evicted for not paying his rent. Aunt Alice had a method of blurting it out which made the observation all the more ridiculous.

3

When I remember Uncle Andrea, Philip's father, I recall a tall smiling gentleman, who used to swing me off my feet in hearty greeting even during my coming-out season at seventeen and who would take Mummie and me to Le Tout Paris and other smart Parisian restaurants.

He was not a particularly rich uncle, I know, yet he was a connoisseur of all the good things of life and he made certain that beside our table, at those restaurants, was always a silver bucket of something on ice.

He was an attentive host and, for my sake, he waved aside the choicest dishes in favor of the plain menu I preferred.

Uncle Andrea was always well-dressed, *soigné*, a man of the world. He treated me with a courtesy and consideration that dissolved my shyness and gaily helped to bring me out.

Glancing around the restaurant with an eye for human odd-

ity, he would notice for my entertainment the delightful absurdities of people, the amusing points of fun. Uncle Andrea
turned everything into a joke.

For example: at St. Moritz a good friend of his, with whom
he was then staying at the Palace Hotel, suffered a bobsleigh
accident. When we next saw the friend, the whole of his head
was swathed in bandages, through which liquid food had to be
syphoned spoonful by spoonful. Uncle Andrea and I took
turns—dripping champagne down the pipe—though we spoiled
the whole atmosphere of our errand of mercy, I think, by shaking with laughter at what we were doing.

Unable to penetrate beneath his banter, I, a mere niece, did
not know that he had once stood on trial for his life. Like Aunt
Alice, Andrea never talked of his darker hours.

In Paris—or was it Monte Carlo?—when the phony war had
begun in 1939, café life was full of controls and stringencies, but
these left Uncle Andrea unruffled.

I remember a luncheon with Mummie when the maître
d'hôtel bent over him with an unusually solicitous air. A consultation went on in a whisper. Then, in the manner of a con-
spiracy, a large coffee cup was brought, from which Uncle Andrea sipped, with twinkling eyes. By now my curiosity was
thoroughly aroused, and I wanted to know its contents. Uncle
Andrea gave me a big wink. His cup was full of impossible-to-
get brandy.

He usually treated Philip in the same mood of indulgent good-
heartedness, joking about my cousin's athletic prowess or youthful escapades. But, as Philip's papa, he would give him advice,
whenever it was sought, with a gentle gravity.

Philip adored his father and, looking back, I can now see
physical resemblances that went unnoticed when I was younger.

Not long ago, leafing through a magazine, I discovered the Annigoni portrait of Philip. I was absently awaiting a telephone call and very naughtily penciled in a monocle and the suggestion of a mustache. I scarcely noticed that I was doodling. And the result suddenly shocked me; for there, in one of his sterner moods, was Uncle Andrea.

Luckily those sterner moods of his were rare. But, at times, I was startled by Uncle Andrea's fiery demeanor, when national topics were discussed.

He was next to youngest of the five sons of King George I, founder of the Royal House of Greece, and could be dogmatic and intense in patriotism. He never forgot, deep down, that he nearly became King George's successor, when the Western Allies were to choose among the sons in June 1917.

As a boy in a multilingual household, I am told, he flatly refused to speak any language but Greek—oddly enough displaying the same stubbornness with which Philip, years later, refused to learn Greek at all.

But how could a young girl know that, for instance, at a crucial point during the Asia Minor Campaign, Uncle Andrea disobeyed a certain command from headquarters, risking execution for treason, rather than following an order he considered detrimental to his native land.

Distilling these memories is almost like reviewing a photograph. It is against the more familiar backgrounds of St. Moritz, the restaurants of the Côte d'Azur and the drawing rooms of Paris that I best remember Philip's father.

In my teen-age ignorance of grown-up perplexities, I never thought it strange that Uncle Andrea stayed at the Travellers Club on the Champs Elysées while Aunt Alice remained at St. Cloud or with her daughters in Germany. When I last saw him,

21

sunning amid the palms and flowers of the Villa Alexandra, his home in Monte Carlo, I was not inquisitive about the lady who was so often at his side.

Uncle Andrea preferred to sit chatting rather than go swimming. At St. Moritz he would walk in the snow, teasing me with snowballs, rather than try the ski slopes with his friend Prince René de Bourbon. Though so tall and soldierly, Uncle Andrea in middle age preferred to sit in the sunshine. Perhaps he knew he had to take things easy.

Uncle Andrea died suddenly of a heart attack in Monte Carlo in December 1944, when he was only sixty-two. He had still maintained some contact with his three daughters, one of whom lost her husband on the Italian front. But the war had severed him irretrievably from his wife and Philip.

His own death came just seven years after the deepest personal tragedy he perhaps knew, the death of his twenty-six-year-old daughter, the Princess Cecile. With her husband, her mother-in-law and her two little boys, who were of course Uncle Andrea's grandsons, she was flying to England for her brother-in-law's wedding, a gay family party, when the plane crashed in flames near Ostend. No one survived . . . and Andrea seemed to lose part of his spirit after that.

4

How did they come together, my Aunt Alice and Uncle Andrea? How did Princess Alice of Battenberg, born in Windsor Castle, and Prince Andrea of Greece, one of the first royal babies of Tatoi, come to be married?

After the lapse of years, I found I had to inquire of my oldest relatives before I could find out the story. And what a story it was—of young love in tight-waisted uniforms and billowing gowns!

At twenty, a young cavalry lieutenant, Andrea went to visit his German cousins at Darmstadt, and there he found Alice, just seventeen, blond and beautiful, finishing her voice education by studying German.

Andrea was a brief and fervent wooer. He followed up his courtship in person with a no less passionate love-making by correspondence. Alice and Andrea wrote to each other once a day, and on one occasion, Andrea even sent five letters.

With such heavy mail dispatched—and answered, beyond his hopes—Andrea finally lost no time writing to Prince Louis of Battenberg for permission to marry the Prince's oldest daughter.

I was often told that Alice's doting great-uncle, King Edward VII, running his hands through her soft ringlets, once declared bluffly that no throne in Europe was too good for her. His consent to the marriage of Alice and Andrea was necessary under the British Royal Marriages Act. It may be, now that he had this responsibility, that he raised an eyebrow at this match with a younger son of a comparatively new Royal House of Greece.

At all events, he stipulated that the bride should be wed according to the rites of the Protestant Church, whatever other forms were required. So in the end the shy Princess Alice was married in three ceremonies, one civil, the second Protestant, and the third Greek Orthodox. She could not hear a word at any of these nuptials, but all royal Europe gathered for a week of such festivities as the little Duchy of Hesse-Darmstadt had never seen before.

Queen Alexandra of England, Andrea's aunt, was the cynosure of all eyes at the Greek Orthodox Wedding in the Russian Church, with her dress of amethyst sequins.

The Czar Nicholas and Czarina Alexandra of Russia were

present as uncle and aunt of the bride. There were dozens of Russian Grand Dukes, a vast contingent of German cousins, aunts and uncles, and even the three-year-old Prince Louis— now my Uncle Dickie, Earl Mountbatten of Burma—led in by his nurse, his noisy chatter drowned in the anthems of the Russian Imperial Choir brought especially from St. Petersburg.

At the time of the Orthodox ceremony, Andrea's brothers Christopher and Nicholas, held golden crowns over the heads of the bride and bridegroom. But, later on, there was an awkward moment for Alice. Unable to see through the beard of the Russian officiating priest, she failed to lip-read his questions correctly: whether she consented of her own free will to marry Andrea and whether she had promised her hand to someone else. In confusion, she loudly replied "No" to the first question, and "Yes" to the second. Christopher's desperate nudges were to no avail.

As at their son Philip's wedding over forty years after, autumnal mists swept around the splendid couple entering their carriage when the wedding breakfast had finished. But the damp evening did not chill the guests. My family records tell of a rush of hilarious royalty under the lamps of the courtyard—followed by an equal rush of stodgy German detectives fearful that the bursting bags of confetti might contain bombs.

At the last moment before the carriage went off, Czar Nicholas succeeded in hitting the bride with a satin slipper which, standing up in the swaying seat, she returned with such a torrent of words that the Czar of all the Russias backed away in the cobbled road shaking with laughter.

For the newly wedded couple, the first years in Greece must have been just as carefree as the nuptials. They lived in the Old Palace which, though draughty and rambling, had an antique splendor.

Aunt Alice added Greek to her verbal accomplishments and, while Uncle Andrea pursued his military career, she began to spend hours at the School of Greek Embroidery, learning painstakingly the intricate stitches, determined to make this national art her own.

Gradually Alice and Andrea's wing of the Palace filled up with babies. Margarita, Philip's oldest sister, was born in 1905; Theodora was born the next year; Cecile arrived in 1911; and, lastly, Sophie was born on June 27, 1914.

The day after Sophie's birth, the shots that set off the First World War were fired at Sarajevo, tearing my aunt's home and all the earth asunder.

Within a few years, more than half the guests pictured in the large wedding photograph were dead.

For the first time Alice found her allegiances were divided, and many family connections severed, by the hostilities. Deaf and vulnerable, she could not easily follow the arguments that built up, through to 1917, between King Constantine and his brothers, including Andrea, over the position of Greece.

Then, that year, Andrea went to London on a mission to assure the British Government of Greece's neutrality and to deny that any secret pact had been concluded with Germany. But in the British capital he was horrified to see newspaper headlines already blazing, "Constantine's Treachery" and "Tino Betrays Allied Plans to the Kaiser." He had hardly returned to Athens when British and French warships began to bombard the port of Piraeus, and then Athens too. With many shells falling around the New Palace, Alice snatched the girls and put them in comparative safety in the Old Palace cellars, in the care of the Queen, my grandmother.

Then followed, in a march of events as certain as the stitches in any embroidery, the abdication of my grandfather, King Constantine, and the accession of his son—my father—to the throne as Alexander I. Within a few weeks, the Allies demanded that Aunt Alice and Uncle Andrea, as well as Constantine, Christopher and Nicholas, go into exile in Switzerland.

Andrea secretly remained on in Athens for a month, aware that as my father's firmest friend he would be needed for support and help. Only when his presence could no longer be concealed did he leave, taking with him a few hundred extra gold francs to aid the others in their plight.

And their plight was serious: scanty travel funds were soon exhausted; the family had to rely on sums borrowed from friends or sent by distant relatives. The pension my father regularly allotted to ex-King Constantine was jealously curtailed by the Cabinet. The household servants who had followed the family into exile worked loyally without a penny in wages.

This hand-to-mouth existence lasted for nearly three years. Then the pattern of everything changed and new designs took shape quickly.

At the end of September 1920, Aunt Alice and Uncle Andrea discovered that they were going to have a baby. But that month came bad tidings too—that my father, bitten by a pet monkey, was seriously ill with blood poisoning.

On October 25, after twenty-nine days of delirium and agony, he died in my mother's arms. A few weeks later, a plebiscite was held in Greece, and King Constantine and his family were restored.

My mother still had three terrible months to endure before I was born, and my birth could, in some measure, offset her loss. Alice, pregnant herself, hurried to her side to give what comfort she could. Though not many of the royal relatives troubled themselves to assist Mummie, in these days of bereavement and shock, Alice would not leave Athens until I was safely delivered.

By Christmas Mummie had already decided I would be named "Alexander" or "Alexandra" in memory of my father—and not "Philip" as he had suggested. In any case, as an expected Prince, I turned out to be a girl when the time came.

In February Alice took refuge herself on the Isle of Corfu at my great-grandfather's summer residence, which had been bequeathed to Uncle Andrea. It was at the villa Mon Repos on June 10, 1921, that my cousin, His Royal Highness Prince Philip of Greece, uttered his first lusty cry.

He was sixth in succession to the throne.

Chapter 2

• 𝔚𝔥𝔢𝔫 𝔚𝔢 𝔚𝔢𝔯𝔢 𝔙𝔢𝔯𝔶 𝔜𝔬𝔲𝔫𝔤

1

THE VILLA Mon Repos has given its name to little houses all over the world, but few of them, I think, have shared its beauty.

My son Alexander spent a summer holiday there only recently, with my uncle, King Paul of Greece, and the Queen, his Aunt Frederika, and Alex described it to me afresh: the road coiling up the hill, the little entrance drive around a magnolia tree, the broad sunny hall, the wide staircase curling up to the upper floor. "There is the sitting room," my son reminded me, "with French windows leading to the garden, and there is the King's study and the dining room and that is all. Upstairs the corridor is painted green, and there are three or four bedrooms, I think, and on the top floor where I slept there are two more bedrooms—yes, maybe they are new. But outside there is no terrace, just a path and two or three steps, and then you can scramble down the rocks and paths about two hundred yards to the sea."

I think that even such a simple description catches the atmosphere of happiness of Uncle Andrea's home, though it does not convey the scent of orange and wisteria or the incomparable loveliness of the gardens around on all sides.

Thick with eucalyptus, magnolia, cypress, olive, orange and lemon trees, the grounds run to the water's edge amid dazzling views of blue sea and sunlit shore. No more romantic setting for the birth of a baby prince could have been planned.

Andrea enjoyed every tranquil moment he was able to spend at Mon Repos. Through the years of exile he fondly remembered it as his only real home. That his son was born there was a particular joy to him, though the pace of events was such that he was away in Turkey, as a corps commander in the ill-fated Asia Minor Campaign, when Philip arrived.

Instead of a proud father, the four older sisters, fifteen-year-old Princess Margarita, fourteen-year-old Princess Theodora, Princess Cecile, aged nine, and chubby six-year-old Tiny gazed down on the child prince in his cradle and begged to be allowed to hold him.

But then a capable English nanny, Mrs. Roose, was employed. "Roosie" was a gray-haired woman who at one time had nursed Aunt Alice herself as well as taken charge of my cousins Olga, Elizabeth and Marina, now the Duchess of Kent. With patriotic faith in her motherland, she brought in quantities of English baby foods and ordered infant woollies from London.

She had scarcely settled down, however, when Prince Louis of Battenberg, Alice's father and first Marquess of Milford Haven, died in England. Hastening to London for the funeral, Alice decided to take along the three-month-old Philip, whom Roosie carried in her arms. Even in the saddened circumstances,

a message on cigarette paper, which he rolled tightly among the valet's cigarettes. In return, using the same method, Uncle Andrea sent out a short note.

Though full of courage, it was clear he felt his position was hopeless. He was charged with desertion from his post and was to be put on trial for his life. The verdict was not in doubt. The new Minister of War, Mr. Pangalos, had visited him only that morning, demanding during an interrogation how many children he had. When Uncle Andrea told him five, Pangalos had said laconically, "What a pity. The poor little things will soon be orphans!"

Leaving Philip and the girls with Roosie, Aunt Alice hurried to Athens, and found every delay and difficulty put in her way.

The King could not help her, for his own life hung on a thread. The Minister of War, though a former school-friend of Andrea's, refused her entreaties. The one mercy he would accord was to allow her to visit her husband in his prison toward the end of the trial.

Aunt Alice sent anguished appeals for help to her cousin, King George V, to her closer Battenberg kinsman, the King of Spain, to the President of France and the Pope. Nearly prostrate with anxiety, she wrote a stream of letters enlisting the aid of every possible member of the family and truly overlooked no one.

Unquestionably Aunt Alice succeeded in arousing the attention of the civilized world. The trials of the alleged seven were, however, nearly over. One by one the defendants were given the merest show of justice and then sentenced to death. The British Government made a strongly worded protest.

Nevertheless, with little time to prepare themselves, the five Ministers were lined up in the prison courtyard and shot.

How horrible that these useless deaths had to occur! The commander-in-chief, who failed in a last-minute bid to gain the sanctuary of the British Legation, was no luckier than the others.

Meanwhile, my Uncle Andrea was arraigned and the personal emissaries of the King of England, the King of Spain and the Papal Legate reached Athens in what had become a race against time.

The trial ended on a Saturday but the court retired without a verdict.

My mother was with Aunt Alice during that awful night of suspense. A crowd waited at the gates of the Old Palace but no news came and the reporters one by one moved away. The judges of the Assembly had, in fact, decided to sleep on their verdict.

It came in the morning—Uncle Andrea was to be deprived of rank and nationality and banished for life. In Paris, his mother, the widowed Queen Mother Olga, was just coming out of the Russian Church when she heard the news. She turned back into the church in tears, crying, "Thank God, thank God!"

Placing no trust in his enemies, Uncle Andrea on his release immediately took refuge with Aunt Alice in the British Legation. Three days later, they went aboard the British cruiser *Calypso*, which then called at Corfu to pick up Roosie with the four Princesses and Prince Philip.

My cousin was then not fully eighteen months old and still so small that the sailors padded an orange crate as a cot in case he should fall out of the bunk.

It is often said that he walked his first baby steps on the deck of the cruiser. At all events it was the first of his many historic voyages under the Union Jack and the sailors who tucked him in could not have guessed that he would one day marry their future Queen, then unborn, and father a probable British King of perhaps the year 2000 plus.

2

Deprived of Greek nationality, Uncle Andrea reverted to the

family line of Sonderburg-Glucksberg-Beck, the line of his grand-father, King Christian of Denmark.

It now proved a blessing that, on assuming the throne, King Christian had insisted his descendants maintain Danish nation-ality. Danish passports were issued to Andrea and his family; and it was under this sponsorship as a national of Denmark that Philip began what one might call his first residence in Britain.

At Marlborough House his Danish-born great-aunt, Queen Alexandra, was waiting to see the eighteen-month-old boy and to approve him. At Kensington Palace, also, the Dowager Marchioness of Milford Haven, his grandmother, took the youngster on her lap, delighted to note the growth and changes of the past six months.

That Christmas saw a happy family reunion—Uncle Dickie and Edwina newly home from their five-months honeymoon, and Uncle George Milford Haven there, who was to become such an important influence in Philip's life. Philip's Aunt Louise was present too, I think, for she did not marry King Gustave until the following year. Among the younger generation was Uncle George's son, three-year-old David Milford Haven, playing with Philip for the first time, and perhaps the Carisbrookes brought Iris Mountbatten, just a few months Philip's senior.

It had been a long time since Kensington had borne such fes-tive company or so many young guests happily content to crawl on its creaking floors.

For a few days the Dowager Marchioness could forget her widowhood, and Uncle Andrea, truly allowed a new lease on life, no doubt kept them all merry.

Next, in the new year, Andrea and Alice were invited by his brother and sister-in-law, Prince and Princess Christopher, to come to New York and to take a subsequent tour ranging from Canada to Palm Beach. There, in one of the largest hotels in Florida, the brothers noted with amusement that the pages sped back and forth through the corridors on bicycles.

During this American journey Philip and his sisters remained safely in Roosie's care at Kensington. The blond Philip went through Kensington Gardens every day, outwardly just another little English boy, pointing at dogs or seagulls and being wheeled exuberantly around the Round Pond by his nanny.

Then more urgent decisions had to be taken. Uncle Andrea no longer received any Army pay, though indirectly he owned an interest in some agricultural property in Greece and had a tiny inheritance from his grandfather. Aunt Alice received an allowance from her brother, but this scarcely met the schooling expenses of the girls. The truth was, they were pitifully poor.

Though Andrea was unwilling to accept too much direct help, one of the chief benefactors, apart from Uncle George Milford Haven, was my Great-uncle George, Andrea's older brother, who had married Princess Marie Bonaparte. Since George and Marie lived in Paris and could be of assistance there, Andrea decided to make the move to the French capital.

George and Marie freely offered a floor of a house they owned on the Rue Adolphe Ivan, by the Bois de Boulogne, to Andrea and the family. Since Marie's ancestors included not only Lucien, brother of Napoleon, but on her mother's side Mademoiselle Blanc of the family which founded Monte Carlo, it is odd to think that the gold francs from the roulette table helped support Andrea's living and were later to pay for Philip's education.

But, even though they knew they had to keep down costs, Andrea and Alice found their new quarters cramped. A small bequest from ex-King Constantine enabled them to enlarge the space a little; then George and Marie came to the rescue again.

George and Marie had built a small lodge on the wedge-shaped property where their personal house stood, on the Rue du Mont Valerien. As this lodge was comfortable, yet had no staff problems, Andrea and Alice were glad to occupy it—amid the apple trees and graveled paths.

For Philip there were still comings and goings from one to another of his relatives. Uncle Dickie Mountbatten recalls an occasion when, at the age of four, the young boy hid himself under a vast bed at Brook House and screamed at being dragged from his private refuge. It was a protest that has always seemed to us to have some point.

3

One of my first memories of Philip is of a tiny boy with his shrimping net, running eagerly, far ahead of me, over an expanse of white sand toward the sea.

Then the scene dissolves and it is another time and the same small boy with ash-blond hair is splashing merrily in the water, refusing to leave it, running and eluding every attempt to capture him.

Long after I have returned to my nanny and the waiting towel, Philip is still there until he is finally caught and taken out forcibly, blue with cold, yelling through chattering teeth.

We were four or five years old when we went to visit my German grandmother, Queen Sophie of Greece, whom I called "Amama" and Philip called Auntie Sophie. She was staying that summer at Panka with her sister, the Landgravine of Hesse; Philip's sisters were there, some well-behaved little German cousins and Uncle Cri of Hesse, whom Philip's youngest sister, Sophie, was one day to marry.

At Panka the smell of the sea was in the breeze. The woods stretched mysteriously beyond the lawns, and the paths led to magical farmyards full of exciting carts on which children could clamber.

There were the same circulation of aunts, cousins and grandparents, the same expeditions to the sea, as there are for my second cousins, the Prince of Wales and Princess Anne, and there will be soon for Philip's newest child, Prince Andrew.

I remember climbing into a huge car for the trips to the seashore. Philip made friends with the good-humored Baltic fishermen and was carried piggyback on their broad shoulders down to their boats, while I scampered alongside. We so loved the sea that we often dashed in fully dressed, before our nannies could locate our swimsuits.

Philip's devotion to the water was, however, outdoors only. Indoors, there was scandalous fun at bathtime when he never wanted to be bathed.

Being the youngest he was supposed to use the tub first and a nightly battle of wits was fought between him and Roosie to see how long he could escape his fate.

When Roosie had him standing only in his vest, she invariably had to bend her elbow to test the water—and that was the moment when Philip dashed wildly from the room.

Through the open door of my nursery I too ran with roars of glee.

Along the corridor, through bedrooms and dressing rooms, this wonderful chase would go. Poor Roosie—who must have been nearly seventy—ran threatening awful punishment while I, shouting wildly with delight, brought up the rear.

Sooner or later, colliding with some grownup, Philip would be captured. But with children's intuition we realized that this bathroom fun gave pleasure to the grownups—all except Roosie!— and this inspired us all the more.

Was it that summer, or was it another year in the timeless world of childhood, that we had such fun at Panka playing with the pigs? That corner of the model farm was a favorite, though forbidden, playground. Philip used to climb to the topmost bars of the hurdles and tight-rope along like a youthful Blondin. If he slipped and fell in the mud, so much the better, because he could then devilishly try to chase me and cover me with dirt.

One afternoon we had the wonderful idea of unbolting all the pig stalls to see what would happen. To our disappointment, nothing changed. The pigs went on grunting and browsing, paying no attention. It was almost as boring as if we were with the grownups on the lawn having tea, listening to the meaningless conversation tinkling over our heads. To stir events up, Philip took a stick to the pigs—and then pandemonium broke loose with a fury of movement and sound.

Squealing, screaming, freed from their sties, the pigs stampeded and scampered past the fodder barn toward the tea lawn.

We could no more control their closed ranks than control the wind. Between the elegant little chairs and tables the pigs rushed, upsetting trays and tea things. I remember aunts and uncles screaming, shouting and running while dismayed servants rushed around, baffled by the swarming tide. It was wonderful while it lasted. Carried on by wild excitement we two, alas, betrayed ourselves.

To this day I remember maintaining, in shameless fear of punishment, that it was all Philip's idea. He made sure it was understood, however, that I shared fully. Happily, Amama understood the experimental urge that moved us. Since the retribution is forgotten, it cannot have been too severe.

Then, near the house, was a big lake on which Philip embarked alone in a little boat when he was no more than six or seven. We were young enough, in any case, to be very much frightened by the hissing swans and their busy broods of cygnets. If we saw a swan nearing us on the path, we would run away madly. "Don't stop!" Philip would urge in panic. "Faster!" I have never known Philip afraid at any other time.

Without a thought of the risks of disaster that made me shudder, he used to climb onto a huge farm horse which he could scarcely straddle, tug its mane, kick his heels and set it going with yells of delight. If he had the chance, he would climb onto a waiting farm cart, haul me up and wildly drive off with it.

Sometimes, in those unchanging sunny summers, we were at Cotrocene, the royal domaine near Bucharest, with my cousin Michael of Romania. He was only five on my first visit, and I do not think I even knew he was Crown Prince; but, by the following years, when his grandpapa, King Ferdinand, had died I was aware that he had been proclaimed King under a Regency.

It made no difference to our play except that there were always many people about: Philip and he and I never quite managed to wander off by ourselves. Michael indeed fully realized he was King and adopted courtly ways early. "I am most pleased with Sandra," he once amused my mother by saying. "She suits me very well."

By now we all had tricycles to try out, up and down the terraces and paths. It was at Cotrocene, I think, that Philip first developed a passion for climbing trees. Riding my own tricycle I screamed loudly one day when a figure dropped from a branch right in front of me. But it was only Philip.

At the height of the summer we were whisked to Auntie Sitta's cool house in the Sinaia hills where I first remember our ponies.

My Auntie Sitta, Queen Helen of Romania, had been my father's favorite sister, and that was an ordered and yet exuberant domesticity about her home. Even now I can see our nannies cheerfully sitting down to tea with bowls of caviar, which was cheaper in Romania in those days than jam.

There were magical rides, too, in a carriage which Michael's grandmother, Queen Marie, used to drive through the fields or lead placidly by the pony's bridle.

One day something fell with a tinkle on the ground and, reaching down to retrieve it, I found myself holding a little crown from the bridle trappings. "You can keep it, darling," Queen Marie said. I did keep it, and cherished it for years, until it was lost with other possessions during the war.

I wish I could say that I gave the crown to Philip, because it would have been so apt a token. But the story, alas, like one of Queen Marie's fairy tales, would only be "imagination real."

Sometimes, when we were walking, Queen Marie would make up her stories. "Now I will tell you," she might announce, "why it is that Philip likes to climb trees . . ." and we would find ourselves carried off into the wonderful realms of make-believe. This world, I am happy to say, has since become familiar to children throughout the world through her published writings.

Although I cannot specifically recall Philip being there, he must have joined us sometimes on those special occasions when we children were allowed to go to Queen Marie's room before bedtime.

In her gorgeous brocaded dressing gown she would sit in an armchair surrounded by her expectant audience. First we were allowed to help ourselves to a big dish heaped with crystallized violets and then, munching rapturously, we would sit at Queen Marie's feet and enter wonderland.

Aunty "Missy" wore full dress for dinner every evening with tiara and diamonds. At times when we knew the meal was to be late, we were up to every possible trick to keep our nannies at bay and stay up long enough for the fairy tales. They were one of the few influences, I think, that kept us out of mischief.

Michael's nanny, Nurse St. John, realized this and used it effectively. At lunchtime, we detested cauliflower and the three of us concocted a protest against the vegetable whenever it was served. With a gleam in his eye, Michael would give the signal and, whoosh, we would upturn our plates simultaneously on the tablecloth.

That evening we would be barred from visiting Queen Marie,

and now I think repentantly of the hours of enchantment all of us lost through cauliflower.

4

When he was six, Philip became a pupil at the Country Day and Boarding School in St. Cloud, which had been founded for children of American businessmen and diplomats in Paris as a progressive kindergarten.

Situated in a rambling old mansion called "The Elms," the school was convenient enough to the house at the Rue du Mont Valerien for Philip to be walked, in good weather, by one of the girls.

When he was old enough to be trusted to go alone, Philip proudly bought himself a bicycle with his pocket money. Each year, from his uncle, the King of Sweden, he had received a pound at Christmastime. He used this as the start of a bicycle fund and, once other grownups heard of it, they increased the fund until Philip found he could make the big purchase.

Philip's first teacher, Donald MacJannet, first remembers him as "a rugged, boisterous boy, but always remarkably polite," adding, "He was full of energy and got along well with other children. He wanted to learn to do everything and even asked at one time to be shown how to wait on tables."

This sounds just like Philip, who has been eager to know how the kitchen works ever since.

With his jersey sleeves darned and a patch on his trousers, he knew at an early age just what he wanted and where he was going. One afternoon, when kept late at school during a heavy rain because his teacher saw he had no raincoat, Philip explained, undismayed, that he was saving his money to buy one and would probably have the garment next week.

Neither Aunt Alice nor Uncle Andrea believed in making things easy. Walking the garden paths at St. Cloud or in the

Bois, his mother talked with Philip of the old days in Greece, of King George I, his grandfather, or Queen Victoria, his great-great-grandmother.

"If you want to know anything about family obligations, ask Mummie!" he said, remembering these conversations years later. His father, too, gently explained the real importance of being a Prince. It wasn't just a name, like being Philip of Greece, as he was known on the school rollcall. To be a prince one had to excel like a prince. To win honor as a prince one had to deserve to be a prince. A prince, in fact, must always prove himself. Such were the first lessons in royalty that Philip ever learned.

Uncle Andrea was aware, it seems, that in the event of a restoration in Greece, King Constantine's sons might at any time be passed over in favor of Prince Peter—or Philip. Against the background of exile there were always these prospects of sovereignty, though the first result of Andrea's kingly preparation in excelling was merely that Philip won a biscuit-eating contest.

On the other hand, Aunt Alice, knowing she could not compete with the prodigality of his American classmates, trained Philip to economize better than other children, so well, in fact, that he even acquired a reputation for being a tightwad.

At the outset he learned to write quickly and always drew very well. Then, for a time, he also picked up an American accent, and would come home singing American football songs.

It was chiefly in sports that Philip developed his new desire to be outstanding. He could swim and dive like a second cousin to a seal; he could box, of course, and Roosie remembers that one day after a disagreement with another boy he returned with a black eye, explaining with delight that his opponent had received two black eyes.

At Panka, in those days, he wandered off alone on expeditions which he thought beyond my scope or beyond the powers of any other children with us, and from these solitary adventures he was apt to return with no explanation and torn clothes, cuts and bruises.

Spending a seaside holiday with King Michael, it was always Philip who staged the hectic pony races over the sands, always Philip who ventured past his depth or who rounded up other boys he met on the beach and organized intensive castle-building brigades.

One August, at Berck, with the children of an old friend of his mother's, Madame Foufounis, Philip staged a fairly typical exploit.

Two of the youngsters were healthy but the third, a little girl with hip trouble, had to spend her time lying in the garden or on the villa balcony.

One day, a beach acquaintance bought toys for the children, all except the little invalid, whose presence was quite unsuspected.

Philip promptly took his gifts to her cot and gave them to her, a gesture resulting in such adult praise that characteristically he hurried to his own room, gathered up every toy he could find and rushed back to heap them all around the girl.

He was never lacking in resourcefulness. One Christmas, when a fancy-dress pageant was to be staged at school, most of the parents made plans for lavish costuming of their offspring. Philip's parents decided he should get along on his own, and he found that he could borrow nothing better than an old pair of trousers. Not to be outdone he blacked his face with soot and jauntily came as a chimneysweep.

One day, he and the little Foufounis boy saw an Algerian carpet seller. Rushing back into the house, they collected all the mats they could carry. A few minutes later neighbors telephoned. Did Madame know the boys were in the street, selling carpets?

As I have said, Andrea and Alice were both inclined to leave the boy to his own devices. One of the reasons was that Alice was busy with Greek embroidery and had begun to help run a shop in the Faubourg St. Honoré.

Legends spring so readily that everyone has no doubt heard the story that this was an antique shop where Aunt Alice tried to eke out a living while Philip played among the priceless crystal vases. In reality, it was a little boutique called "Hellas," where Greek embroideries, tapestries, medallions and other articles were sold for the benefit of Greek refugees—a charitable enterprise.

Princess Marie would send her friends to the boutique; in distant New York Princess Christopher of Greece, the former Mrs. Nancy Leeds, impressed it on her acquaintances, and the place flourished. Sometimes, equally to good purposes, Uncle Nicholas sent his pictures there for sale, and I believe my cousins, Elizabeth and Marina, helped from time to time in the stockroom.

Often my Uncle Nicholas would speak of "the bitterness of being deprived, above all, of one's native land." But in Paris in those days there were so many cousins and uncles, so many arrivals and departures of the Hesse family and Mountbattens, that for one so young as Philip there was never real awareness that his father and he were exiles or were out of place.

His life seemed like any other child's. For three happy years Andrea would take him to see the store windows at Christmas or perhaps set him riding on the children's railway in the Bois. Sometimes, Uncle George and Andrea and their friends indulged him with ice cream at a café.

And I am sure that as time went on and Prince Godfrey of Hohenlohe-Langenburg came courting Margarita, his oldest sister, the usual tickets to the movies were forthcoming as a ready means of getting an irreverent younger brother safely out of the way.

Chapter 3

• The English Schoolboy

1

"THINK OF Philip," I was told. "He doesn't mind school. He wants very much to go to Cheam."

When we were both nine, Philip was sent to boarding school, at Cheam in England, and I—much less willingly—advanced to Heathfield School. While I was an ineffective and unhappy pupil that year, Philip was to find all the fun—and challenge—as an English schoolchild that he hoped for.

There were reasons for his going to prep school in England then. Andrea, recognizing that a restoration of the monarchy in Greece was unlikely, felt that Philip should be prepared to earn his own living. He dismissed the idea of an army career for him, partly because of his memories of the bitter end of his own soldiering.

Ultimately, Alice's family put pressure on Andrea for an English education, abetted by Philip's personal feelings. The one or two Christmas visits Philip had made to Lynden Manor, invited by his Uncle George and Aunt Nada Milford Haven, convinced him he wanted to be in England.

In contrast to my own long-lived dislike of boarding schools, Philip derived real pleasure from Cheam—never better shown than when he chose the school for his son, Charles.

When Philip first went, his letters to me were filled with excitement about the school diving contests or broad jumps. I do not recall, though, there was much word about the academic subjects. There was plenty of news about young David Milford Haven, and Uncle George, who never failed to come to Cheam on parents' or relatives' days and who always sent his car for Philip and David to bring them home at mid-term.

Since so much has been written about Uncle Dickie Mountbatten's influence on Philip, I would like to set *Uncle George* in italics.

When Philip first arrived in England, Uncle Dickie was on naval maneuvers in the Mediterranean, and it was Uncle George who in fact entered Philip at Cheam and assumed the role of second father.

At first, Philip had begun his residence with his grandmother at Kensington Palace. But he enjoyed playing a jazzy saxophone which disturbed his great-aunt, Princess Beatrice, who felt that the Palace was the wrong place for the younger generation. Philip was quickly accepted at Lynden.

Here, Uncle George paid no heed to the racket that lively schoolboys made. He had a garden barn, converted into a badminton court, where Philip and David made all the noise they wanted. George himself was modest and quiet, with an inventive turn of mind. He told fascinating stories of the naval battles of Heligoland and Jutland. He left the Navy to enter business not long after Philip's coming—but there is no doubt that he was the first to turn the boy toward a seagoing career.

Meanwhile, Philip and David grew up together. On one holiday, Philip came to Paris from Lynden with half a tooth missing, and he explained with his usual grin that he lost it in a head-on whack with David playing hockey.

On one adventure, the twosome bicycled down from Lynden to Dover to a Boy Scout camp and arrived so saddle-sore they were determined to hitch a more comfortable ride home.

At the Dover dock, a huge barge was loading with grain to sail up the Thames to the port of London. The other Scouts and an understanding scoutmaster were an irresistible force. When the encampment was over, the two Mountbattens and the others boarded the barge, stuffed themselves with rations of rock cake, and spent two days and two nights sailing, sleeping on sacks of grain in the hold.

This was between terms. At Cheam, Philip quickly won the all-school diving championship and was still not twelve when he tied for first place in the high jump. When we heard he was also good at soccer, it was almost anticlimactic.

In classes, Philip was really good in history but when he won the form prize in French, I demanded to know why there wasn't a handicap. Philip was sheepish; he knew he had profited from all the years he had lived in Paris.

When Philip next came home for the holidays, he went to St. Cloud. He found the family there beginning to split up. He seldom saw his father, and the girls had their own preoccupations. Marriage was in the air.

Sophie, the youngest, whom we all called Tiny, was the first, when she married the tall man whom I called Uncle Cri, Prince Christopher of Hesse. She was only sixteen.

Next, twenty-year-old Cecile married Prince George of Hesse-Darmstadt, and the expense of that wedding had scarcely been paid when Margarita, in her mid-twenties, married Prince Godfrey of Hohenlohe-Langenburg. Lastly, the family nuptials were rounded off when Theodora married Berthold, the Margrave of Baden. This wedding soon had consequences for Philip's own life.

Theodora's father-in-law, Prince Max of Baden, in his family home near Lake Constance in Germany, had founded a school, with the far-reaching goal of training youths in the tasks of national and European recovery.

Prince Max, who died too soon to be influential as one of Philip's "uncles," was a humanitarian who had emerged in the days of the 1918 Armistice negotiations to become Germany's first post-war Chancellor. When he retired several years later in favor of the Socialist Ebert, he felt strongly about the need for a new—and unorthodox—kind of education for the younger generation. By 1933, Salem School, which he had begun with his own son Berthold and three or four other boys, had grown into one of the foremost in Europe.

Theodora thought that Philip should attend it, not only out of respect for her new family relationship but because she felt that Aunt Alice, now entered upon her religious work, needed the reassuring presence of her son close by. Philip was now twelve years old. Once again a family argument developed—this time whether he should continue his training as an English schoolboy or be brought up as a student in the liberal Germanic tradition.

Salem won, though Philip probably disliked the change because he had been having too much fun in England.

In the fall of 1933, Philip entered his new school. The curriculum was tough, yet calculated to encourage precisely those qualities of physical fitness and self-reliance which he had already displayed.

Before breakfast, Dr. Kurt Hahn, the former headmaster, relates: "all boys ran 400 yards, and at night did physical drill. Four times a week, academic studies in the mornings were interspersed with running, jumping and javelin throwing."

In addition, there were heavy construction tasks, including the building of a cinder running track and even the erecting of a concrete jetty into the Bodensee.

The precepts of Salem education, it was explained, meant the genuine shaping of a boy's character, "through self-discovery and self-effacement in a common cause, by periods of silence to train imagination, by making games important but not predominant, and in freeing him from an enervating sense of privilege as a son of wealthy parents." Perhaps no goals could be better in the upbringing of a prince.

But Philip did not exert himself more in schoolwork than was necessary to avoid trouble. He probably did not enjoy Salem. Merry or melancholy he always showed his feelings, and I knew that he really longed to be back in England.

Matters soon grew more serious. The liberal ideals of the school clashed with the rising Nazism, a menace which Philip then found only ludicrous. One day he caused an angry official to come to the school by laughing in the streets as some storm troopers paraded. He was in even worse trouble when the Nazi salute became compulsory.

In England an upraised arm has meanings for a schoolboy quite the opposite of political and, whenever he encountered the salute, he would jibe at it regardless of admonitions to caution.

Abruptly, when Philip had been at Salem less than a year, it was decided he should return to England to Uncle George. "We thought it better for him—and also for us," Theodora explained at the time.

2

The letters that Philip sent my way from Gordonstoun were few and far between but into these rare scraps there crept new names, "Old Hahn," and "Chewey," and "Lewty," the nicknames of his masters.

Philip first went to this newly founded school in Scotland in the autumn term of 1934 and he found it like another Salem, transferred to Britain and enhanced by a nautical flavor.

This milieu suited him to perfection, and Kurt Hahn, who had come to Gordonstoun from Salem himself, took an immediate liking to the boy. "When Philip came to the school," he wrote, "his most marked trait was his undefeatable spirit. He felt the emotions of both joy and sadness deeply, and the way he looked and the way he moved indicated what he felt. That even applied to the minor disappointments inevitable in a schoolboy's life. His laughter was heard everywhere. He had inherited from his Danish family the capacity to derive great fun from small incidents. In his schoolwork he showed a lively intelligence. In community life, once he had made a task his own, he showed meticulous attention to detail and pride of workmanship which was never content with mediocre results."

The Gordonstoun system, one might add, did not need Philip to put it on the map. Kurt Hahn had gained the approval of Claude Elliott, then headmaster of Eton, Lord Allen of Hurtwood, Lord Tweedsmuir, and others, who were its mentors.

Situated a mile from the sea, stately Gordonstoun House was already associated with royalty through its former owners, the Gordon-Cummings family.

It is often said that Philip helped build the school; and he did, very literally, in a team of boys which began the conversion of an old stable building into dormitories and classrooms for the ever-increasing influx of new pupils. And Philip soon became a room leader, a role that tested his reliability in leadership at an early age. He found that he was to be taught to supervise himself. Every evening he had to make entries on a chart, declaring whether he had followed certain simple rules, such as "not eating between meals," or "taking two cold showers." He vigilantly kept to the rules—but no one ever inspected the chart.

Of course, I heard of japes and scrapes, just as I do from my own boy at Le Rosey today.

A dreamy biology master, on one occasion, was drawing on the blackboard, concentrating on his illustrations so deeply that he failed to see nearly every boy in the class stealthily leaving the room by the window. After some twenty minutes spent sunning on the bank of the school lake, his pupils, having proved their temerity, all crept back, still undetected.

Another master must have found his life miserable when Philip and other boys sewed up his pajamas, filled his shoes with water and subjected him to every possible practical joke until they decided at last that he had had enough.

Probably his worst jam occurred when Philip, cycling like a young maniac to the seamanship classes at Hopeman Harbor, nearly crashed into a carriage containing a baby, and avoided disaster only by his remarkable agility. Though he tried to appease the mother with profuse apologies, complaints were made—and Philip called to account.

But he was "often naughty, never nasty," as Kurt Hahn recorded, and his seamanship instructor, Commander Lewty, soon listed him as "a cheerful shipmate . . . very conscientious in carrying out both major and minor duties . . . thoroughly trustworthy."

While I was at finishing school in Paris, I did not see Philip for more than a year, but Uncle Andrea used to visit me at the Hotel Crillon, bringing the news.

Absurd photographs were shown of Philip peeking from behind a potted plant in a nativity play, or looking super-tough in hockey or rugger kit. I learned with astonishment that was qualifying to be a coastguardsman; nothing on earth would have induced *me* to spend a night in a fisherman's hut. But Andrea always spoke of Philip with pride. "What do you think now?" he would ask with a twinkle. "Philip has been building a pigsty and has promised to send me a photograph!" Or he would say, "I have had another school report!" and he would try to hide his pleasure, looking at me very hard through his monocle.

Then, in November 1936, Andrea had a happy reunion with his son at the otherwise solemn occasion still known in the family as The Funeral. The Monarchy had been restored in Greece the previous year when my father's older brother, my own Uncle Georgie, came to the throne. It was decided that King Constantine and Queen Sophie, and my great-grandmother Queen Olga, who had all died in exile during the republican years should be brought from the crypt where they had been interred in Florence for reburial in the family ground at Tatoi and that they should lie in state for six days in the Athens Cathedral.

The procedure had a macabre touch, but it was a great and sorrowing tribute to the old Royal Family and for all of us it could not help but be a joyous reunion. Aunts, uncles, cousins and all the kith and kin arrived to drive through streets decked with flags and lined by cheering people, just a few days before the darker drapes of mourning were hung. The whole of the Hotel Grand Bretagne was taken over to house us, and Philip, of course, was given special school leave to enable him to be there.

I gazed in amazement at my handsome fifteen-year-old cousin. He had suddenly shot up. He was thin without being gangling, and, wearing his first dinner jacket, he rather set out to impress us.

He told me that he had sailed the North Sea in complete charge of a cutter with oars or sails, and that he thought he might be cruising to Norway soon. And there was a badge for climbing, running and lifesaving that he intended to win.

"What would you like made in iron?" he urged one of my uncles. "I'll build it for you. We do this ourselves at the smithy in the village."

Here was a new, up-and-coming member of the family to please and interest some of his elders. At one lunch, when family estates were under discussion, Uncle Andrea said with a droll air, "He knows about estate management!" And it seemed indeed that Philip was fast becoming an all-around young man.

Only a discreet A.D.C. and I later knew how hopelessly he disgraced himself. The evening before the final funeral service, we all attended a big dinner party, at which there must have been something wrong with the lobster. The next morning everybody felt ill, and no one was in worse shape than Philip, who had eaten a good deal. Luckily, he was released from the duty of many of the older men of the family, to walk through the streets in solemn procession behind the triple cortège. But the car ride undoubtedly did Philip no good.

In the Greek Orthodox Church the congregation stands throughout the service and there are no pews or hassocks as in

55

other churches. As the solemn anthems pealed through the cathedral and eighty bishops, gathered from every town in Greece, took up their positions with slow dignity, Philip and I retreated to a shadowy and inconspicuous position beside some pillars. "Sandra," he whispered, in mixed agony and terror. "I'm going to be *sick!*"

As with his dinner jacket, he was wearing the first morning coat and carrying the first top hat of his life. I could only suggest that the top hat might be a good bowl. Fortunately, he resisted this suggestion and managed to survive, so to speak, through the obsequies.

I was almost beyond helping him, seeing only the funny side of it, shaking with uncontrollable giggles behind my black mourning veil. But I did manage to draw him closer to the pillars, where he could lean back. Then we emerged in the sunshine and took our places in one of the cars.

Philip's pallor increased as the procession began, and then suddenly he leaned forward and seized his topper just in time. I think I successfully masked him from the view of the crowds. But there remained the terrible riddle of what to do with the top hat. I am afraid that the simple solution, to leave it on the floor, never occurred to us.

As we left the car, at the Palace, Philip caught the eye of an A.D.C. with a look of despairing entreaty. I hope that the aide felt sympathy at the ordeal of a schoolboy at a funeral, when he found the noxious topper thrust into his hands.

On the other side of the picture, this great gathering of all the branches of the Royal House of Greece kindled a torch in my cousin's impressionable teen-age mind, as it did in mine.

The Salic law had removed me irrevocably from the line of succession, but Philip may have noted a deference on the part of some of the officials he encountered, a slight indication that he was by no means remote from the throne himself.

His own father had stood with Nicholas, Christopher and my Uncle Palo as Guard of Honor at the triple bier. Philip's imagination was caught by the pomp and panoply of royalty as never before, and he cornered one of our aunts in a room, asking so many questions that she had to beg him to stop.

For the first time, he wanted to know precisely who was who. He sought to have relationships defined and dated. Unfortunately his mother, who had always been the great authority on family genealogy, was not present—away ill, I think, in a nursing home.

It must have been on another, later occasion that, arriving unexpectedly at Aunt Alice's house, I found Philip seated at a desk, looking very grown-up and serious. The look he gave me made me ask what he was doing. "Oh, I'm looking at my father's birthday book," he explained.

Yet there was a touch of pride in his tone. Perhaps it was then that Philip realized fully the *aging* of his father's whole generation.

My Uncle George, with his walrus mustache, and balding Uncle Nicholas and lean, bald, Uncle Christopher must all have seemed to him, as they did to me, incredibly old men.

In the next generation, there was only King George II followed by his bachelor brother Paul. Then there was Uncle George's son, Prince Peter, also a bachelor at the time, and next in succession, startled by the hitherto little-considered possibility, came young Prince Philip.

When Philip later asked questions of his grandmother, the Dowager Lady Milford Haven, at Kensington Palace, she no doubt had much to say on the mystique of royalty, telling him her creed, so natural in a granddaughter of Queen Victoria, that kingship is a healing force in the world.

She liked to stress the importance of sons and grandsons of kings proving themselves again and again in a free trial of strength. Perhaps she satisfied Philip's curiosity with stories of the life of her husband, Prince Louis of Battenberg. All this could only underline the constant counsel from Uncle Andrea that it was indeed up to Philip to do better than other boys.

Soon Uncle George Milford Haven began sending Andrea school reports showing that Philip was applying himself very strictly in academic work. He was doing specially well in mathematics and geography, which Uncle George may have hinted to him were of importance in a naval career. He was one of the school's best in modern languages.

We all began to know with more certainty at this time that Philip would be a sailor. When the school schooner *Henrietta* did cruise to Norway, Philip was on the expedition. His commander reported, "He is now one of the most efficient members of the seamanship guild."

Despite that lobster trouble, Philip apparently had the tough kind of stomach that went with a good pair of sea legs. Long after other boys were in their bunks he was still on his feet, with a grin. But there was one unavoidable penalty for standing the rough passage on a ship's deck—he was made cook.

3

Renewing the neglected associations between cousins, the family brought us together again soon, with the wedding of my Uncle Palo, then Crown Prince of Greece, to Princess Frederika of Brunswick.

This was truly a royal occasion for our own generation: Prince Peter, King Michael and Prince Philip were to be the three best men at the wedding.

Michael, Philip and I were all sixteen, and I was to have my first real evening gown. I was so transported by this thought that I do not recall much of the actual ceremony, except that Peter and Michael held crowns over the bride and bridegroom, and Philip served as an attendant.

The night before the wedding, a big dinner party was held at the Palace and I found myself seated at Philip's side.

"I'm ravenous," he said, and began to eat most of the food served to me as well as his own.

"Keep your asparagus for me!" he commanded. But the Palace servants, always proud of their superb service, were more on their toes than ever that night. Half the guests found their dishes whisked away almost before they could lift their knives and forks.

I noticed my Uncle Christopher holding on determinedly to his plate with thumb and forefinger, while he ate American style with one hand. Indeed I became so fascinated by his dexterity that a footman took my asparagus before I could give it to Philip, and my cousin was furious.

He declared he would get back at me. His opportunity came when we were all standing around with champagne glasses near the buffet, and my Aunt Helen's bare back presented an irresistible target.

Philip glided up silently and pressed his cold champagne glass on her skin. Aunt Helen whirled around but Philip was gone. He had acted so quickly that I don't think he had realized whose back it was. We differ about that to this day, but I, poor innocent, was victimized with a torrent of indignation that might be expected from a Russian Grand Duchess.

After the wedding came a week of picnics and family parties which Philip and I very much enjoyed. My cousin, I found, now had a dashing air—and I soon learned why.

At school he had already captained the cricket team; he was expected to be captain of the hockey team; and the chances were he would represent the school at the Scottish Schools Athletic Championships. He was quite proud—and he did, in fact, go on to take all the honors.

Yet, at the time of Uncle Palo's wedding, though Philip did not talk of it, there was some chance he might not return to Gordonstoun.

Considerable pressure was then being put on Uncle Andrea to enter Philip in the Greek Nautical College. Hints were cast, possibly, that Philip's progress in the Hellenic Navy might be smoothed. This consideration, however, did not move either Uncle Andrea or Philip.

Andrea's good humor masked the memory that his native land had disowned him; even when conditions altered, he wanted to cut his relationship with it. And Philip, in addition to his independent spirit, had established ties in Britain that—once more—he did not want to surrender.

Not only was school satisfying to Philip, but his favorite environment was British, at the home of Uncle Dickie Mountbatten. He would talk to me excitedly of Uncle Dickie's imaginative improvements, from the fastest elevator in London to the dining room that could be made into a movie theater. Or of Uncle Dickie's study, where he could pore over the relief map of the world that hung on the wall.

He felt strongly, too, about the fun he was having with David and many other acquaintances.

Since Andrea had no wish to dissuade the boy from his self-chosen course in Britain, he fell in readily with the plan that Philip would return to Gordonstoun. It was agreed then that he would take the competitive special entry test for the Dartmouth Royal Naval College—Britain's Annapolis—with the possibility of his transferring later to the Royal Hellenic Navy.

Chapter 4

◦ Seventeen in Venice

1

IN HIS LAST terms at Gordonstoun, Philip was head boy or
"Guardian" of the school. This was quite a remarkable position, obtained purely on merit by one in a hundred. Before he
could be chosen for it by the headmaster, he had to be elected
to a body of "Color Bearers"—a sort of upper house—by his own
fellows.

Uncle Dickie once tried to put into my muddled head a simple
explanation of how Philip had done it step by step: first as a
room leader, then as a captain in nominal charge of a department, and next as one of the ten "helpers" each of whom had
real charge of a department (such as games, or seamanship or
practical work).

Philip's "helper" department was, naturally, seamanship. He was now firm friends with the Hopeman fishermen, and I think on one occasion he was allowed to accompany them on an all-night fishing trip. As a senior boy, the curriculum left him two free afternoons a week. Philip loved to spend this spare time pottering around the harbor, or clambering about the schooner, the two-masted *Prince Louis*, named after his Battenberg grandfather.

Sight-seers who came looking for Prince Philip of Greece were sometimes surprised to find a jerseyed, untidy-looking boy scraping the barnacles off a hull, polishing a ship's bell or engaged in some other menial task.

What did they expect, I wonder? One woman asked for an autograph, and Philip was too polite not to oblige. His sense of absurdity overcame him, however, and hurriedly scrawling something he thrust the book back into the applicant's hand. Before the scribbled signature could be made out as "The Earl of Baldwin," he had climbed to the top of the topmast and was safely remote.

"Prince Philip's leadership qualities are most noticeable," Dr. Hahn reported, "though marred at times by impatience and intolerance. He is a good school guardian, feeling deep concern about the unwritten laws entrusted to his keeping."

And strangely, Dr. Hahn also noticed Philip's unusual ease and forthrightneess in dealing with people of all kinds. Though the break-up of his true family background might be considered an unhappy influence, he made up for it in a diversity of social contacts and experiences available to few youngsters of his age.

Already the discomfort and hard living of a cruise on the *Prince Louis* around Cape Wrath was contrasted, on holidays, with the semi-pomp that Princess Theodora maintained as Margravine of Baden. The creaking stairs of Kensington Palace were equally in contrast with Uncle Dickie's high-powered elevator at Brook House with its brilliant passengers.

A minor adventure occurred at Kensington Palace when a policeman, ordering Philip to come down off a roof, was met with defiance.

At this time, Philip could almost have qualified as a cat burglar for, at Lynden, he and David used to canoe downriver after dark and clamber to a roof skylight to enjoy the jazz sessions at a local hotel.

The Foufounis family were in London too, giving Philip insight into more placid domesticity. He would sometimes go around to their little flat in Bayswater, and help with the dishes in the kitchen.

When the oldest girl, Hélène, was to marry, Philip suggested he might give her away though he had to borrow a morning suit for the wedding. Some years later he became godfather to her children and helped place one of the boys at Gordonstoun.

At the school itself his personal friends were by no means confined to a top social set. They included the son of a Dundee shopkeeper and the son of a Scottish railwayman, today both captains in the British Merchant Navy.

As school "Guardian," Philip helped build a coastguard hut to watch the wild coasts of Morayshire, and organized and headed a special Gordonstoun group of coastguard watchers.

Kurt Hahn recalls when he first suggested building the guard hut to Philip, he encountered passive resistance: the young man had suspected that this was another enterprise aimed at the good of his soul.

But when Philip found that His Majesty's Coastguard Service was prepared to aid, and even pay for the telephone, he immediately recognized the reality of the job asked of him and saw to it that the hut was built, in the thick of the autumn gales, ready for the worse weather to come. Henceforward the Gordonstoun coastguard station was manned by the boys during every gale warning.

And then, before he knew it, another term drew around to a summer close and Philip's Gordonstoun days were nearly over.

"Prince Philip is universally trusted, liked and respected," Dr. Hahn said in a final school report. "He has the greatest sense of service of all the boys in the school. Prince Philip is a born leader, but will need the exacting demands of a great service to do justice to himself. His best is outstanding; his second best is not good enough. Prince Philip will make his mark in any profession where he will have to prove himself in a full trial of strength."

2

My mother had invited Philip to spend his holiday with us in Venice that summer, but the prospect alarmed my Uncle Andrea. "Philip still has to pass his exams," he wrote. "Whatever you do, keep him out of girl trouble."

Mummie thought this request a little absurd. Philip to her was still just a schoolboy, much too young for even a mild flirtation.

That first evening she decided it would be nice for the three of us to go to the Taverna della Fenice where two or three wandering musicians played. But Philip was quite unimpressed by this atmosphere. He downed his spaghetti, obliterated the fish, quickly put away a huge steak, disposed of the fruit and then suggested over the coffee, "Let's go on somewhere!"

Philip gave me an impression at the time of a huge, hungry

dog; rather like a friendly collie who had never had a kennel of his own and responded to every overture with eager tail wagging.

There had been Kensington Palace and Lynden Manor and Brook House, I know, and yet there was the sense of complete homelessness.

Though he was never sorry for himself, to be fed and looked after meant such a lot to him, and he responded to Mummie with an affection that at once won our hearts. He was immensely gregarious, so ready for each new experience.

But in the mornings, I used to think that Gordonstoun had utterly exhausted him. He used to lie in bed until eleven or twelve o'clock, refusing every invitation to come out into the garden.

Then he would come down demanding a full English breakfast of eggs and bacon, from our Italian cook, which had to be done particularly as he wanted. Afterward came lunch and then he was ready for exploits. He was delighted to find that I had a speedboat and went off in it alone, leaving me stranded, for hours at a time.

I exasperated him sometimes when I wanted to sit at home while he wanted to go out. Mummie's garden is on an island, bounded by a canal on one side and a lagoon on the other, with a swimming pool and nine acres of wandering paths—surely all the heart could desire. Couldn't he get a chair, I suggested, and finish *Busman's Holiday*, the book he was always talking about? But Philip wanted to get on the move.

One afternoon he fixed a vine stake as a mast in our rowboat, the *Johnny Jones*, then borrowed a tablecloth from Mummie and ran it up as a sail; in this primitive craft we set off to sail to Torecello. It took all afternoon and I am sure that Philip's seamanship alone got us there. Since he did not feel up to sailing this makeshift boat home, we returned in a friend's launch with the boat in tow.

Another evening Philip took command of a friend's sail boat, which he was convinced he could handle better than anybody else aboard. This may have been the case in open water but it was not in the narrow twisting precincts of the Venice canals—and he did look a bit worried until we returned safe to the dock.

Of course, Philip and I saw only the funny side of everything, and we laughed continuously at all the incidents of the summer.

Venice soon provided the occasion of probably the first and only time Philip ever got drunk. At Gordonstoun he had to promise abstinence from alcohol and at royal wedding parties he never more than sipped champagne. Released from this vow, I imagine he had to have one night out.

Lord and Lady Melchett, always the most understanding of friends, were giving a party at one of the fishermen's *taverna* that had become fashionable at Torcello. It was an evening of music and laughter, but almost before we knew what was happening the Italian wine went to my cousin's head. He began to make us all laugh by dancing around the terrace like a young faun, a very handsome and graceful faun, I must admit. Then, fired by our enjoyment of his antics, he began swinging from the pergola. Then it went beyond a joke, for the pergola collapsed, bringing the vine down with it, and Philip disappeared under the greenery. The enraged proprietor and his daughters—and a rueful, sobered Philip—cleaned up the mess. Happily, the Melchetts did not mind paying for the damage.

By now, of course, Mummie had set her bush telegraph working, and my handsome cousin was never short of invitations to parties and dances.

Sometimes I went along, but more often I preferred to bury

myself in a book, while Mummie and Philip departed by the speedboat or gondola.

The Count and Countess Volpi in their lovely palazzo on the Grand Canal, the Count and Countess Castelbarco, the Count and Countess Andrea de Robilant, Prince and Princess Chavchavdze, Mrs. Millicent Rogers, Mrs. Cobina Wright and the indefatigable Mrs. Corrigan were some of the hosts and hostesses whose hospitality and gaiety enlivened Philip's seventeen-year-old summer.

At eleven o'clock or so Mummie would murmur that she wished to go. But there was invariably some lovely young thing in tulle or organdie to whom Philip suggested they should give a lift home. "There's no need to keep the driver, Auntie Aspasia," he would say. "I'll take over. The boatman's had a long day." Amused with his guile, Mummie would comply, but not without stipulating that he should be back in the house within twenty minutes. And however unwillingly, he had to obey.

Blondes, brunettes and redhead charmers, Philip gallantly and, I think, quite impartially squired them all. He used to love having people in and they seemed to be different people each time. Then gradually one girl in the group began to stand out a little more than the others. Since she lived not too far away, Philip was deprived of his usual evening excuse. "Auntie Aspasia," he begged on one occasion. "It's such a lovely night. Let's stay out a little longer, after you've gone in!"

Mummie was aware of the heady perils of Venice and the moon and the sirocco. "Very well," she agreed. "But you are to cruise round and round the island and don't stop the engine! I will be listening!"

We were both listening, in fact, as the motor launch came lazily chugging across the lagoon, then sounded fainter and then throbbed down the canal. It died away and then the noise crossed the lagoon, faded at the point and came down the canal.

But after three or four circles had been made, the *put-put* of the motor suddenly stopped. There was five minutes of silence— which we filled with surmise—before we again heard the steady *chug-chug-chug*. Another loop or two were accomplished, and then again a few minutes of silence. . . .

"We had trouble with the spark plugs," Philip sheepishly explained the next day.

Mummie was fully reminded of Uncle Andrea's plea that Philip should be kept out of girl trouble. Was Philip seeing too much of this one girl? Was her mother inviting him too often to bathing parties at the Lido, picnics and *en famille* parties at the more romantic dance restaurants? I found that Philip did not like being teased about it and perhaps I was the only one who could afford to tease him. But when he began taking her out in my speedboat while I stayed at home, we had a most uncousinly row.

And then I must confess that I got together with a friend, and she and I concocted a little plot. We pitted guile against guile. My friend was an attractive sloe-eyed creature who knew precisely how to oppose the magic of the moon, the cry of a gondolier, the soft splash of water in the lagoon. She deliberately set out to fascinate Philip. She flirted with him atrociously. She flattered him, charmed him—and one must admit that she twisted Philip around her little finger strictly according to plan.

She both wove and shattered the spell of Venice, that age-old enchantment. By the end of the summer David Milford Haven arrived for a fresh whirl of fun, and we were again a happy, heart-whole little group. More important still, Philip returned to England to work hard in his special entry exams, to be placed

first in two subjects, and Mummie and I raised our glasses when
we heard he had successfully passed.

3

As a joke, David had a huge brandy glass specially blown at
Murano to take home to his father, so enormous that it was like
a bucket.

Mummie and I knew his father was not well but little knew
how seriously ill he was. Almost before the summer ended, Uncle George died of cancer. He was only forty-six. It was still
not a year since Dr. Hahn had called Philip to his study to tell
him of the tragic death of his sister Cecile. Philip had taken it
like a man. Now, in an equally swift and unnerving stroke, at a
crucial phase of his career, he lost the uncle who had so long
been closer and more encouraging than any foster-father.

There was now no Uncle George with whom to discuss a
probable exam question. David was already in the Navy and
Lynden seemed terribly sad and empty. Philip knew he had to
win through purely on his own merits, and giving what solace
he could to Aunt Nada, he settled down for an intense term
of study.

For a time he went to Cheltenham to live with Mr. and Mrs.
Mercer, a naval coach and his wife. Mr. Mercer found with
pleasure that the boy was eager to get on. Apart from Saturday
night visits to the movies, and radio or record sessions with the
daughter of the house, Philip kept to the grindstone. His allowance seemed to the Mercers to be especially limited, and they
found him not a difficult boy to control.

In attempting to enter Dartmouth under his own steam,

Philip had the disadvantage of competing with younger boys who had entered direct from prep school. But he passed the special entry exam, placed a medium sixteenth among the thirty-four successful candidates and, early in 1939, wore a cadet's naval uniform for the first time.

I will not attempt to trace Philip through the Royal Naval College at Dartmouth, a man's world so unknown to me. Uncle Andrea received encouraging reports that his son was working hard and behaving well. It was as if Philip felt an inner urge to justify himself, first to the father whom he so seldom saw, and second to the fond memory of the uncle now beyond his reach. Within a few months my cousin had the satisfaction of winning the King's Dirk as the best all-round cadet of his term. "I cannot but be pleased," he wrote.

Promoted as a cadet captain, he passed each stage of accomplishment with the same ease as Uncle Dickie Mountbatten, and with considerably more facility than Uncle Bertie (King George VI) nearly thirty years earlier.

Uncle Bertie had undoubtedly heard a lot about Philip before that rainy summer day of July 22, 1939, when the royal yacht *Victoria and Albert* dropped anchor in the Dart and the King and Queen, the two Princesses, Uncle Dickie and others landed at the College steps.

It has so often been said that Philip and Elizabeth first met at the 1937 Coronation or perhaps at a children's party. Although innumerable parties were held at Brook House for Pammy and Pat Mountbatten, the fact remains that both Philip and Lilibet cannot remember any earlier meeting than Dartmouth, and even this has gained a public significance they by no means share.

Not long ago, when she was ill, Lilibet watched on television a ceremony which Philip was performing at Dartmouth and she confessed to a friend that the buildings in the background looked completely unfamiliar. How could it be otherwise? For Lilibet the College had been just another setting that seemed of no special consequence at the time.

It all started, in reality, because many of the younger cadets had become victims of a twin epidemic of mumps and chicken pox. Uncle Bertie planned to attend a morning service in the chapel with his wife and daughters when the College doctor intervened. Owing to the risk of infection, he felt it wiser that the Princesses should not go.

Instead Lilibet and Margaret went to the pleasant red-brick Captain's House, home of the Dalrymple-Hamilton family.

It was my Aunt Elizabeth, now the Queen Mother, and Uncle Dickie who put their heads together and soon hauled Philip out of chapel to help squire the two little girls.

Philip rather resented it, I believe, a lad of eighteen called to help entertain a girl of thirteen and a child of nine. But he politely said, "How do you do?" munched ginger crackers, drank lemonade and then suggested, "Let's go and have some fun. How about a game of croquet?"

Years later, as they tried to recall this occasion, I heard him affectionately joking with Lilibet. "You were so shy," he said, "I couldn't get a word out of you."

He was a little nonplused as he talked to the blushing princess. He suggested the croquet lawn as a social escape hatch but, to his horror, both little Margaret and Miss Crawford, the governess, came too.

"How good he is," Lilibet said admiringly afterward. Poor Philip was relieved when chapel came to an end and he could relinquish these duties.

Uncle Dickie, however, steadfastly procured his nephew an invitation to lunch on the royal yacht, where Philip contributed

73

to the conversation mainly by teasing Margaret and laughing a good deal.

That afternoon they inspected the swimming pool and the College grounds. In the evening when all the cadet captains were invited to dinner aboard the royal yacht, Philip found that Lilibet still observed a nursery schedule and had not stayed up.

The next day, however, they met again at lunch and tea, and everyone in the family soon knew that Dickie had encouraged the boy to show off. Philip very much wanted to make a good impression, even though some members of the party thought his manners off hand. His real opportunity came when it was time for the royal yacht to sail away.

As a College tribute, many of the cadets followed it from Dartmouth Harbor into the Channel in rowboats, sailboats, motorboats, any craft they could find. One by one, they fell behind as the yacht stood out to sea, all except Philip. I can easily imagine that he deliberately missed the signal to return. At last he alone was left, approaching. Lilibet took the glasses to crane for a last glimpse of him.

"The damned young fool!" Uncle Bertie told Sir Dudley North. "He must go back. We must heave to otherwise and send him back." The final orders to return had to be shouted at Philip by megaphone until at last he dipped first one oar, then the other, and turned around. He told me afterward that he had only been trying to show his utmost respect for the King.

That was how it all began.

Chapter 5

❖ A Prince at War

1

WHEN PHILIP completed his first year at Dartmouth, he won
the Eardley-Howard-Crochett Prize as the best cadet of the
year. But then the naval authorities had an awkward problem.

The difficulty was that Britain was not at war with Germany,
while Philip's native Greece was neutral. Philip had proved
his worth as a seaman, and his kinship to Lord Louis Mountbatten, commanding a destroyer flotilla, meant that he had important sponsorship. How was he to be assigned?

On Uncle Dickie's advice, Philip took the initiative and tried
to be naturalized as a British subject. But it turned out that the
necessary legal machinery for naturalization had, like many
other ordinary procedures, been suspended for the duration of
the war.

We heard from Aunt Alice that she had approved a plan for Philip to remain in the British Navy rather than enter the Hellenic Navy but that Uncle Andrea could not be consulted. Contact with Philip's father, owing to the war, was indirect and uncertain.

Meanwhile, Uncle Dickie managed to stir Philip's superiors, who were tending to put off a decision on the adventurous but neutral and royal midshipman.

In January 1940, Philip was assigned to the battleship *Ramillies*, then at Colombo in Ceylon. This was a suitable compromise inasmuch as the Indian and the Pacific Oceans were then perhaps the least active areas of operations.

The *Ramillies* soon escorted the troop convoys from Australia. Philip, though destined to be boisterously welcomed by millions fourteen years later, first arrived in Australia an unknown foreigner. He made the most of his two shore leaves as a midshipman by seeing as much of the country as possible. He even got to a cattle station in Queensland where, I have heard, he spent three or four days working as a jackaroo, or apprentice cowboy.

Then the *Ramillies* returned to Alexandria, Egypt, an extremely active base from which the Admiralty hurriedly transferred the "problem prince" to British East Africa.

Philip joined the cruiser *Kent* in May and left for the *Shropshire* at Durban, South Africa, in September. Here he enjoyed the wonderful, inexhaustible hospitality that the people of Durban give to every sailor on shore leave, being whisked through a melee of parties, dances, jungle car excursions and even sample nights on safari. These early glimpses into his wife's future realm were varied—and important.

Just at this time I was in Italy, living through days of suspense until, on the afternoon of October 28, 1940, the Greek Ambassador telephoned Mummie with the news that Italy had invaded Greece.

With members of the Greek Embassy and relatives of the Royal Family, I was on the last diplomatic train to travel across Yugoslavia to Athens. Uncle Dickie, for his part, must have lost no time sending off telegrams reminding the Admiralty that his nephew, Philip, was no longer a neutral. Thirsting for action, my cousin was promptly sent to the battleship H.M.S. *Valiant*; he had not been aboard three days when she took part in the fleet bombardment of Bardia.

Then, suddenly, Philip turned up in Athens, gay, debonair, confident. After a stay in a hotel, Mummie had with some difficulty found a house near the Lycabette. There was no place on the hillside to park a car, and we used to toil up and down, groaning. But Philip would come bounding up the hundred steps, read for fun—for record-playing and dancing—with a whole new group of friends.

There was Ronald Fleming, of the British Legation, I remember, and John Beith, now an ambassador, and Aubrey Moodie, Joan Palairet and many others.

Happily, Uncle Andrea's old cook had come out of retirement to help us, jubilant to be in royal service again. Sometimes, he used to peek through the door at Philip, whom he had last known as a little boy, marveling and murmuring happily to himself. Philip attacked his dishes with gusto, saying that they tasted like old times, but I don't think he ever realized the former servant was with us. We were probably too engrossed in other topics to mention it.

In the evenings the family often gathered either at the Palace with the King (Uncle Georgie) or at one of our homes.

We never knew whether Philip would join us. When the air

raids began we were supposed to go to a shelter which a thought-
ful government department had provided deep in the cellar.
Instead, on the first night we went up to the roof garden and
watched.

I was alarmed next day when Mummie showed me the silvery
chunks of shrapnel she had found close to where we were standing. Yet this seemed to dismay none of the others in our lighthearted group and the next raid found us again on the roof, this
time with Philip, who contributed a running commentary amid
the bark of the ack-ack guns, the flutter of searchlights and roar
of the bombers.

But Philip never talked naval shop or said a word about his
personal naval duties. He would accept a dinner invitation, saying, "Maybe I can come," and this was the only assurance we
had. One evening my punctilious Uncle Georgie was unusually
late for dinner, and told us that every available plane in Greece
had been bombing the Italian fleet; it proved to be an episode
in the Battle of Cape Matapan in which Philip took part.

The bombing had followed the discovery by an R.A.F. flying
boat of a division of the Italian fleet steaming southeastward
across the Mediterranean.

By night the British battle squadron had sailed up full speed
to intercept a group of enemy cruisers. Philip was in charge of
a vital battery of the *Valiant*'s searchlights on her engaged side,
and his task was to illuminate the Italian ships *Zara* and *Fiume*
as soon as the enemy closed. It was my nineteen-year-old cousin's baptism in battle—the Italians did not get off one shot, and
three-quarters of the thirty-odd rounds fired by the *Valiant* were
direct hits. The *Zara* and *Fiume* lurched helplessly.

Though this was war, within a few seconds Philip's searchlights were scouring the ocean for survivors. He was mentioned

in Admiral Sir Andrew Cunningham's dispatches and his commander, Admiral Sir Charles Morgan noted, "Thanks to his (Philip's) alertness and appreciation of the situation, we were able to sink in five minutes two eight-inch gun cruisers."

Yet, Philip never told me a word of any of this in our later hours of conversation. When he was awarded the Greek War Cross and I congratulated him, full of curiosity, he simply shrugged.

The strange happenstances which linked our lives together were still present. Just four weeks later I was myself under fire, diving into the cover of wheatfields beneath the shadows of Messerschmitts, lying face down amid the shriek of machine-gun bullets that I can hear to this day. When we flew out of Greece to safety, from Souda Bay to Alexandria, Philip was somewhere on those blue Mediterranean waters upon which we gazed wearily.

In Alexandria, there were air raids but there were also kindly, hospitable friends. I was once in a restaurant when it received a direct hit, and I had wondered only a few seconds before whether it was wise to get under the table and spoil my white frock. As everyone did, we lived through the perils of war in a mood of gaiety. Uncle Dickie arrived, urbane and smiling in white, but furious because he had lost a dressing case of gold-backed brushes when his destroyer *Kelly* was sunk under him, after a direct hit from a thousand-pound bomb.

Smiles threaded nearly every day-to-day event. Uncle Georgie reached us safely; his ship, the destroyer *Decoy*, was escorted by the *Valiant* with Philip in its crew. Then, one morning, Mummie and I were at breakfast when we heard a familiar whistle and outside our window Philip and David shouted to us with whoops of glee.

I had not seen David since Venice. I had to admit to myself that I had been worrying about Philip. Now we were all three together again, ready to do the town.

We went out to a swimming pool and splashed happily in the sun. Philip had contrived to get hold of an incredibly small car and in it we streaked through the streets with the noise of a thousand demons.

For the first time I found my two cousins handsome and attractive beaux, very useful at taking me around. I liked David's lazy smile and Philip's broad grin, and I was unhappy at leaving them behind when Mummie and I were ordered to move to the comparative safety of Cairo.

But Philip soon tracked us to Shepheard's Hotel. In his little wasp of a car, he and I went out to the Ghezire Club, swam, or just talked through the long lazy afternoons when he was off duty. We explored the old bazaars and the magnificent botanical gardens, or in a chatty mood went to Groppi's for tea.

Philip used to talk, even at this time, of a home of his own, a country house in England he had planned in his mind to the last detail of fixtures and furniture. This was so like him: always planning precisely where he was going, and what he wanted. We then spoke of Aunt Alice, who had refused to leave Athens and had occupied herself with the care of some twenty orphans at Uncle George's house.

Philip did not think the Nazis would disturb her inasmuch as his sisters were married to Germans. He was philosophical about his mother's decision. There was no news of Uncle Andrea in Monte Carlo. But, after all, the war could not last very long. . . .

When Mummie and I embarked at Port Said in the *Nieuw Amsterdam* to sail to South Africa with the King, Philip came to the dock to see us off. He was due for a promotion and thought he would soon be returning to England. But we were all delighted and astonished when, after only a week or two at Groote Schuur, General Smut's home near Cape Town, Philip turned up there, having been transferred to a troopship which practically followed in our wake.

Philip was, however, on his own itinerary during that short shore leave, more than in Alexandria. He wanted to see as much of the country as possible and, since Freddy (the Crown Princess Frederika) had a car, he went off with her exploring the Cape Province, while Mummie went riding, and I joined up with other friends.

2

Sitting at my desk every morning, seeking to mingle my memories and my notes of Philip's career, little incidents come into significant focus. One evening in Cape Town when I wanted to chat, he insisted on finishing a letter he was writing and I, cousin-like, asked, "Who's it to?"

"Lilibet," he answered.

"Who?" I asked, rather mystified.

"Princess Elizabeth, in England."

"But she's only a baby," I said, still puzzled, as he sealed the letter. Aha, I thought, he knows he's going to England and he's angling for invitations. But, as it turned out, I was doing my cousin far less than justice. The gentle assurances and recognitions of the heart, had they already begun?

Philip soon left Cape Town on a ship for Halifax to pick up Canadian Army units. It was to prove a memorable voyage. En route at Puerto Rico the Chinese stokers deserted.

All the midshipmen, Philip still among them, were paraded and ordered, "Volunteers for stoking."

83

Through the glutinous heat of the Caribbean, Philip sweated half-naked in the stokehold, doing his turn of five or six hours. It made a strange contrast, I reflect, Philip shoveling coal while, in England, a King's daughter perhaps thought of him in her castle. When it was over, Philip was given his certificate as a qualified boiler trimmer; today it has a place of honor among his cherished souvenirs, which include a Grecian lucky medallion, his father's signet ring, a pennant from the destroyer *Whelp*, his own Coronation program and the receipted bill for his wife's bridal bouquet.

After the embarkation of the Canadian troops, Philip's ship completed its journey to England. I reached Liverpool from Cape Town toward the end of September 1941, and I seem to remember that Philip again arrived at the same place at about the same time.

He was to spend the next two years on home stations. At first, in our spare time, when we could put the war behind us, we had plenty of fun together. Mummie and I stayed at the sandbagged Ritz Hotel for a while and then we found an apartment of our own in Grosvenor Square. Philip would come to lunch, full of plans for a night out at the 400 Club or the Savoy. My cousin Marina, the Duchess of Kent, invited us all to Coppins, where the autumn leaves were scurrying over the lawns; it was less than a year before her married life was to end.

Sometimes, David Milford Haven made us laugh by treating Philip with naval superiority. Soon, though, we learned that Philip was to be promoted to sub-lieutenant, with nine months' seniority out of a possible ten. This was an award on sheer merit, recognizing that he had passed his course with four firsts and a second.

While taking the course, Philip was one of the minnows at

Whale Island, the naval gunnery school. Then he "went to Scotland"—which was all we could be told.

In reality, Philip was appointed to the *Wallace,* a flotilla leader of the destroyers operating out of Rosyth, achieving his ambition to serve on a small ship, even though the *Wallace* was a leaky tub nearly thirty years old.

Constantly running the gauntlet in the East Coast convoys of 1942, he was promoted to second lieutenant in July and first lieutenant of the *Wallace* in October.

For once, the gossips were all wrong in attributing this quick climb to Uncle Dickie, who was always writing his nephew reams of instruction and advice, to which Philip seldom had the chance to reply. This time the promotion was made at the express request of the captain of the *Wallace* and, at twenty-one, Philip thus became the youngest officer in the Navy to hold the highly responsible position of senior executive in a ship of that size.

But, of course, I best remember Philip on furlough, dining and dancing and confiding, and his afternoons of talk with David in chilly Kensington Palace. Just as a part of my "war duty," I used to go to see the boys there to cheer them up. For Kensington was like living in a warehouse—the chairs in most of the rooms covered with dust sheets, the dark shadows on the walls outlining paintings put in storage, even the carpeting replaced by threadbare and shabby rugs.

But I was not alone in trying to lighten this somber background. Right in the middle of the mantel, in the place of honor, was a Christmas greeting with the signature "Lilibet."

The card did not sparkle like something on a Christmas tree, as perhaps it should have done. Only time and memory bring this afterglow. I learned later that Philip had sent Lilibet a Christmas card from Athens in 1940 and the ever polite Princess was alarmed when she discovered that he was not on the family's holiday mailing list. Long into the New Year she bothered Uncle Bertie to send a return card. "As long as he gets it I don't mind," she wrote. After that she carefully chose the card for Philip herself.

Historians who like to date precisely every phase of affection may find me unhelpful at this stage, for I was so ardently busy with my own thoughts of King Peter.

Among the strange similarities between Philip's life and mine, romance came to us both about the same time. And for us both there were the wildest difficulties and obstacles to overcome before we settled for happiness.

When Peter went to Cairo in readiness for possible Allied landings in the Adriatic, Philip left England for the Mediterranean.

No doubt my letters to Peter and Lilibet's letters to Philip traveled on the same planes, if not in the same diplomatic pouches. One of Peter's letters to me, with his scrawling "I zaz you!" his sweet silly version of "I love you," was carried in the British Foreign Minister's—Anthony Eden's—dispatch case, and Philip's letters to Lilibet, I know, traveled by equally direct routes.

Diplomats, couriers and service liaison officers were our winged Cupids. Peter, however, was away for a long eight months. Philip returned in November 1943, when his ship put in for a refit, and he did not go to sea again for four months.

On his well-earned leave, between instructional courses, he was invited to Windsor for Christmas. That was the time he saw the two princesses play in the pantomime "Aladdin," and he entertained the King with a half-comical account of adventures off Sicily when German aircraft dive-bombed his ship—without a single hit—for half an hour. In the drawing room, after dinner, the lights were extinguished and they all sat around the fire to listen to ghost stories.

"We settled ourselves to be frightened," Margaret wrote later, "and we were *not*. Most disappointing!" But was it so disappointing to Lilibet and Philip, close together in the shadows for perhaps the first time?

Behind drawn curtains at the Villa Alexandra that same night, Uncle Andrea dined with his friend Jorgens Bagge, the Copenhagen department store owner, and two or three other people. "Don't you remember . . . ?" these friends of Philip's father reminisced with one another.

I went to the tailor's with Philip one afternoon while he was fitted for a new uniform and half-expected to be invited out for tea. But, suddenly, he had to dash off. "Who is it?" I challenged, naming first one young adorer and then another; he had the good grace to blush.

Mothers liked to "fairy-godmother" him for all they were worth. When Philip had a severe bout of flu, it was no surprise to find him recovering in a suite in Claridges belonging to a family which had shown him a great deal of kindness.

I sat by his bed and reproached him for not seeing enough of Mummie and me, while he cheerfully plucked the grapes some other person had sent him and ejected the pips at me with naval accuracy.

But soon, first at one house, then another, I heard the wail, "Where's Philip?" I knew, however, that he had been at Coppins and had had a heart to heart talk with Marina.

One young lady who telephoned for him at Kensington Palace was definitely told he was away. She would have done better to call the small house Uncle Dickie had taken at 16 Chester Street, where Philip had moved into an attic bedroom as a hideout.

Full of thoughts of my marriage, I twice saw Philip lunching at Claridges and merely nodded across the room. One day, just before our wedding took place, Peter and I went to tea with Uncle Bertie and Aunt Elizabeth at Windsor.

The conversation was happy and confiding. Aunt Elizabeth is so motherly and she puts a person at ease so quickly that there was none of the tense atmosphere of mustn't-say-this-or-that, none of the polite absurdities so frequent in Palace homes.

Peter and I spoke of our hopes and plans for married life. We all talked of Marina who would be coming out of mourning for the wedding, of Uncle Dickie and Uncle Georgie, and skimmed through the usual huge round of news of uncles and cousins. But Philip was never mentioned.

On my wedding day, Uncle Bertie served as Peter's best man and Uncle Georgie, King of Greece, came to the consecrated room at the Yugoslav Embassy to give me away. There, apparently, Uncle Georgie took advantage of a romantic occasion to speak warmly about Philip and Lilibet to Uncle Bertie.

Uncle Bertie simply could not believe that his daughter had fallen in love with the first eligible man she had met. She was not yet eighteen, and Philip only twenty-two. He promised to consider the matter—the two Kings were great friends—but soon he advised Uncle Georgie: "Philip had better not think any more about it for the present."

3

From May until August 1944, Philip continued his training and did miscellaneous duties for the *Whelp*. He was anxious, during this period, about becoming a naturalized British subject in order to make his commission in the Royal Navy permanent.

Uncle Dickie tried to secure some quick action and advanced Philip's case to the King. Uncle Bertie correctly advised that Uncle Georgie, as his liege King, should first be consulted. Uncle Georgie gave his royal consent in the early fall but by that time Philip had been sent overseas.

The *Whelp* escorted the *Ramillies* to Algiers and, afterward, to the Straits of Bonifacio, in readiness for the invasion of southern France.

For a few hours, as his destroyer steamed eastward across the Mediterranean, Philip was closer in this world to his father than he was ever destined to be again. But then the *Whelp* continued via Malta and Suez to Ceylon, where she joined the 27th Flotilla under Admiral Somerville, and shortly was incorporated into the British Pacific Fleet, based in Australia.

Just as South Africa was to be the testing time of the heart for Lilibet at twenty-one, so Philip found Australia at twenty-three.

With a golden beard, he hit feminine hearts, first in Melbourne and then in Sydney, with terrific impact. Now taking part in the dangerous attacks on Japanese-held islands, he naturally wanted to enjoy his leaves as fully as he could.

Yet with all girls he aimed at one objective: non-involvement.

Philip was no longer oblivious to gossip. If awkward rumors arose he insisted, sometimes rudely, on scotching them immediately. On one occasion, he returned from a ball to a friend's house with a young blonde in tow. They all sat and talked for a while and then it was noticed that Philip had quietly fallen asleep.

It was getting late and the girl became concerned because her mother was waiting up for her. Rather than wake an obviously tired-out lieutenant, the friend took her home. They had no sooner left the house than Philip opened an eye and smilingly offered the friend's mother, Mrs. Fallon, an explanation. He had seen that heads were turning and nodding in his direction as they left the ball. If he had taken the girl home, there would have been an even bigger story for gossips.

Daughters of publishers, steel heiresses, girls with huge department-store and farming fortunes all crossed Philip's path.

But it was Lilibet to whom he patiently wrote his "letters home." Many girls flung themselves aggressively at Philip. But it was the timorous, secluded one in England who had captured his heart.

Philip left Australia in the summer of 1945 when, after a refit in Melbourne, the *Whelp* and her sister ship *Wager* were assigned as escort to the *Duke of York*, flagship of the fleet.

When the Japanese collapsed, the *Whelp* and the *Wager*, with the *Duke of York* and the *Missouri*, flagship of the American Admiral William Halsey, became the first Allied ships to sail into Tokyo Bay. Later Philip was one of the British officers transferred to the *Missouri* for the famous surrender ceremony on her deck that brought World War II to an end.

Chapter 6

"Rocks in Uncharted Seas"

1

FIRST FROM Tokyo Bay, then from Hong Kong, Philip's letters winged their way home.

Just after V-J Day, my son Alexander was christened in the Chapel Royal of Westminster Abbey; I received belated congratulations from Philip on his birth. Lilibet was the baby's godmother and held him during the ceremony with a worried look of responsibility. It was to be the last family service that she would attend at the Abbey until her own wedding two years later.

Meanwhile, Philip was having a final overseas fling.

In Sydney, one day, he borrowed a Land Rover (a vehicle similar to an American Jeep) from the Governor General's residence, but since the vehicle had the Royal Crown insignia instead of number plates, every policeman saluted it and held up the traffic to let it pass at intersections. This didn't suit Philip at all.

He stopped using the Rover and rented a small car at a garage instead. Yet even this led to difficulties. When the necessary papers were signed, the garage proprietor wouldn't accept the single word, "Philip," as a signature. My cousin complied more fully with "Philip of Greece" and the proprietor grew belligerent, convinced that this Limey customer was pulling his leg.

It all took a lot of readjustment. These two little incidents symbolized the future of Philip, I thought. Through the war years, he had so gladly shunned the constant problems implicit in being royal. Now they again piled around him and he was confronted gradually with a mountain of procedure which he had to bear with, detail by detail, as if he were taking a complex naval course.

The *Whelp* returned to Portsmouth early in 1946, and for the last two months of her commission, Philip was put in command.

Then, in London, he moved into Uncle Dickie's house in Chester Street. He carried in his luggage his first small box of decorations. Among his campaign stars and citations were the Greek honors my Uncle Georgie had bestowed: the War Cross, the Order of the Redeemer, second class, and the Order of St. Constantine and St. George, fourth class, with swords.

For his long-awaited, joyful reunion with Lilibet, Philip first drove to Windsor with Uncle Bertie. They found plenty to talk about on that journey. The twenty-five-year-old naval officer was not the raw boy the King had encountered before. "I like Philip," he commented. "He is intelligent, has a good sense of humor and thinks about things in the right way."

I know that my own husband in his twenties was often a little in awe of Uncle Bertie, and so I suspect that Philip also suffered from "nerves" this time. For him, so much was at stake.

But perhaps both Uncle Bertie and Philip kept away from talk of weddings, though the coming marriages of Pat Mountbatten to Lord Brabourne and Andrew Elphinstone to Vicary Gibbs were in the air. There was the question of Philip's naturalization.

After speaking with Uncle Bertie, Uncle Dickie had unremittingly urged the case and pushed it to the point of discussions at the level of Prime Minister, Foreign Secretary and Home Secretary.

Also, my Uncle Georgie's mere assent, as King of Greece, was not enough. The internal political situation in Greece was so unsettled that he could not be sure of returning to his throne, and (it was pointed out) the naturalization of a member of the Greek Royal House as a British subject was sadly liable to be misinterpreted. Some cautious officials even felt that naturalization might indicate the willingness of a royal prince to become a refugee.

An incident reminiscent of Philip's problem comes to mind when Peter and I went to have tea with Uncle Georgie in the royal suite at Claridges.

With his tea the King always insisted on having a little homemade jam which was specially made for him by a friend. But in order that the precious jar should not be removed by hotel servants Uncle Georgie invariably hid it away—and then forgot where.

We searched with him high and low, behind books, potted plants and curtains, inside an ornate clock case and in cupboards. "It's about as difficult as finding a way for Philip," the aide-de-camp remarked, with an amused glance at us.

2

Poor Philip had other troubles. He was no sooner home than it became necessary for him to go quickly to Monte Carlo to settle his father's affairs.

My dear Uncle Andrea had lived there during the war, accepting gratefully whatever news filtered through of his daughters and grandchildren and learning indirectly of the tides in Philip's affairs.

On his doctor's orders Uncle Andrea took things easy, for he had been warned that his heart was not strong. But he saw the rejoicing of liberation when the American forces landed in southern France, and he was permitted to join a jubilant party with American friends in Nice.

In his own jaunty way, he saw the opening of the brave new world that we all expected. Then one night—it was just before dawn on December 3, 1944—he got out of bed and donned his dressing gown, seated himself in his armchair and quietly died, meeting death itself like the great gentleman he always was.

With the fullest honors that the little Principality of Monaco could render, and with detachments of the French Army saluting him, he was taken to rest in the Russian Orthodox Church in Nice.

At that time, of course, nearly everyone on the Riviera was existing on credit, so the Greek Consul General paid the funeral expenses. It was nearly two years later that Philip went through his father's possessions, opening his luggage to find suits moth-eaten in storage and many sad souvenirs. "He took it philosophically," a friend recalls.

When all commitments were met, including provision for certain dependents, no estate remained. A memorial service was held in the Russian Church, and the clergy in tribute to Prince Andrea and his son conducted it in Greek. The honor of these final ceremonies, however, needed no translation.

At Marseilles, the coffin was carried aboard the Greek armored cruiser *Averoff* and placed on the self-same plate where the bodies of King Constantine and Andrea's mother and grandmother had rested years before.

With royal salutes Andrea was taken to the family cemetery on the hill under the whispering trees at Tatoi. There a simple stone was cut:

ANDREA VASILOPAIS (Son of a king)
Prince of Greece
Prince of Denmark
1882-1944

3

Aunt Alice endured the German occupation of Greece and the civil war that followed it. The Germans had respected her neutrality and the occupation was mild compared to the horrors perpetrated later by the Communist-inspired guerrillas who sought to seize power.

During the bitter fighting in Athens, gas, electricity and water were cut off, and the most meager quantities of food or a bucket of water meant long treks. A friend remembers seeing Princess Alice returning alone through the darkened streets with an empty bag. She had been out by herself, heedless of the risk of snipers, in the pathetic, endless search to feed the orphans whom she still tended.

A hospital colleague moved heaven and earth to have Aunt Alice receive extra Red Cross parcels. After many appeals this food finally arrived. But Aunt Alice adamantly refused to take it.

In despair, her friend secretly bought food on the black market but still had to be careful that Aunt Alice never knew where it came from. In a sense, the terrorist laws were merciful when they forced Alice and Aunt Helen, the Duchess of Kent's mother, finally to leave Greece.

As a still happier result, Aunt Alice was one of my first visitors—apart from Peter, of course—when my son Alexander was born in July 1945.

First Uncle Georgie sat beside me for a while, then Aunt Alice came. She was in the full flow of one of her talking moods, and chatted for hours on more aspects of baby care than I ever knew existed. She looked at my baby with more than usual admiration. "He is like you," she said, "and that means he is like Cecile." I caught in her eyes the haunting thought of the daughter she had lost.

In Philip, too, the same touch of sentiment made him keep and wear one or two of his father's old suits when he returned from Monte Carlo, and to have the ivory handle of his father's old shaving brush freshly bristled so that he might use it every day. Even the picture of Lilibet he carried around was in a battered leather frame which had belonged to his father.

When the first rumors of a royal romance began to circulate, it was denied, so gossips assumed that an understanding existed but was being kept secret. In reality, this was not true. If Philip had already made up his mind, he had not yet taken the irrevocable step of proposing, and shy, sensitive Lilibet had not spoken her own intimate thoughts.

Peter and I had had a house at Sunningdale during the war with its own private gate opening onto the Windsor Great Park, and, when we left it, Uncle Bertie told us were were still welcome to walk in the park and woods whenever we wished. It was always so nice to escape from London for a while that we often made this a favorite occupation on weekends. And we found we had company.

Once, when we didn't even know Philip was in England, we met him walking there with Lilibet and Margaret and their cousin, Lord Elphinstone.

We exchanged greetings but asked no questions: it was still wartime and not polite to ask questions. Another time, two of the royal corgis dashed through the bracken and when we looked around expecting to see Uncle Bertie and Aunt Elizabeth, it was

Philip and Lilibet, walking alone. They were so lost in conversation that we decided not to bother them, so we just waved and went on.

They seemed relieved to be left in peace. I lifted an inquiring eyebrow at my husband. "Could be," said Pete, reading my thoughts. "But for goodness' sake . . . they're only out for a walk."

This, however, was the first of several encounters. We used to see them holding hands, disengaging themselves until we came closer and they could see it was only us. Few people wander in the Home Park and it was an idyllic setting.

"I only hope Philip isn't just flirting with her," I once told Marina. "He's so casual that he flirts without realizing it."

Marina said soberly, "I think his flirting days are over. He would be the one to be hurt now if it was all just a flirtation or if it is not to be. One thing I'm sure about, those two would never do anything to hurt each other."

"Well, let's hope they don't have to wait as long as we did for their engagement and wedding," I replied.

"They will probably have to wait much longer," said Marina. And she added with a smile, "I won't be able to influence Uncle Bertie for Lilibet nearly as easily as I did for you."

Marina was always a good keeper of secrets. She did not tell me that Philip and Lilibet sometimes came for lunch when there were no other guests. Philip, on the other hand, really didn't bother about hiding anything.

After his home leave, when he was assigned to H.M.S. *Glendower*—which isn't a ship, as it sounds, but a naval shore establishment—he used to write his letters at a local hotel and address them boldly to "H.R.H. Princess Elizabeth, Buckingham Palace." There was none of the subterfuge for him of letters addressed to an intermediary. And he simply gave them to the night porter to mail.

But the wedding of Andrew Elphinstone to Vicary Gibbs, Lilibet's lady-in-waiting, was a family occasion that in itself fanned rumors. Practically every member of the Royal Family went to the reception afterward at the Savoy Hotel, and one of the wedding cameramen caught a beautiful picture of Lilibet and Philip standing together for all the world like a bride and bridegroom.

Every newspaper in the world used the picture. Wearing her bridesmaid's wreath of orange blossom and lily of the valley, Lilibet was holding her bridesmaid's bouquet. Uncle Georgie appeared in the original photograph also, but I think all papers, without exception, cut him out!

That summer of 1946 Philip was invited to Balmoral and then the tide of world gossip knew no bounds.

4

Balmoral has not many guest rooms; unexpectedly they all seem to be on the ground floor, and I rather think that Philip had the same room that my husband occupied during his first visit a year or two before. And Philip, too, must have been startled to find the nearest bathroom a block away down the corridor and the nearest "other accommodation" even further down at the end.

Philip and Peter must have shared the same first impressions of the white-washed lobby, the overwhelming array everywhere of antlers and stag's heads and even hides hung like tapestries on the wall.

Philip seems to have had the same big brass bedstead with a lacy brass lamp sprouting from the wall above his head. Quite a lot of the bedroom furniture was brass, though the heavy metal-work of the huge washstand had been painted white.

Like Peter, he must have been astonished by the old-fashioned plumbing that had survived at least two or three reigns. There was still no running water in the bedrooms and servants brought hot water—the brownish peat water of Balmoral—in polished cans.

More startlingly Victorian, the enormous toilets had mahogany armrests and basketwork lids, with a handle you had to pull upward till with volcanic gurgles everything went "whoosh." Yet they all contributed to the period charm, like the profusion of tartan doilies and mats, the tartan rugs that covered mysterious chests in the corridors, the statues of Albert and the serene paintings everywhere of Scottish landscapes and Landseer dogs.

Then, Philip was initiated into the activities of the typical Balmoral day . . . the appalling deerstalks when one trudges for miles and miles into the hills behind some dour and determined gillie.

Philip had to fight off the swarming flies and mosquitoes. Like Peter, I think he, too, borrowed Elizabeth's rifle to bag his first deer.

Philip however was spared the first wartime shock of finding that having killed your deer you have to carry it home yourself, slung from a pole.

For Philip, a pony carried it to the road. There he found a chauffeur waiting and saluting, and he sank exhausted into the plush luxury of the limousine, to be driven home.

At dinner at 9:15, Uncle Bertie was in black tie and kilt, and kilts were preponderant among the other guests, most of them neighbors. And Philip was surprised when, after eating, fiddles, piano and bagpipes struck up in the sitting room and space was cleared for Scottish reels!

Yet, as I say, Balmoral has its great charm as well as its absurdities and quaintness: the music of the rushing streams, the sheer beauty of the Scottish countryside. Here, at last, Philip and Lilibet could be truly alone . . . and Philip proposed.

"Beside some well-loved loch, the white clouds sailing overhead and a curlew crying just out of sight. . . ." Lilibet described the scene in a poetic phrase.

But I am afraid that later, when Philip talked seriously to Uncle Bertie in his study, there were still many difficulties to overcome. The idea of an engagement was tacitly accepted but he was advised to wait, at least for six months and maybe more, before it could be made public.

For Philip, in fact, had to accept the same ambiguous unofficial engagement, with all its secrecy and complications, that had befallen Peter and me.

Whenever Philip married, he primarily wanted to continue his naval career. First he had been advised to wait for naturalization until the Greek monarchy was restored. Now, Uncle Georgie was actually back in Athens as King, but still he was told to hold off. The argument now was that it would be unhelpful to the royalist cause for a Greek Prince to renounce his nationality so soon *after* the King had returned to the throne!

In addition, there was the question of Philip's rank and civil status. Should he become a commoner? Precedents dating back to 1886 were researched before Uncle Bertie agreed with Uncle Dickie and the Prime Minister that he could grant him the title "His Royal Highness, Prince Philip."

But with a determination that decidedly pleased the King, Philip said that he greatly appreciated His Majesty's offer but that when he became a British subject he would prefer to be simply "Lieutenant Philip, R.N."

When it was decided that he had to have a surname, Philip suggested "Oldcastle," an Anglicized version of Oldenburgh, from which the Danish Royal House had originally sprung. But this was chewed over by a dozen genealogical and heraldic experts and then rejected.

There could be no shadow of dispute on Uncle Andrea's estate, so a judge's opinion was sought in the Chancery Division in the case of "Rehder versus H.R.H. Prince Philip of Greece." Mr. Rehder was one of the lawyers concerned with settling the estate.

Another difficulty was the constitutional requirement for a prospective husband of Princess Elizabeth to be of the Protestant religion. Happily, it was decided that this could be satisfied simply by receiving Philip into the Church of England shortly before the wedding.

Faced with this obstacle course of formalities, Philip plodded on patiently. Returning from his Balmoral leave, he was transferred to the H.M.S. *Royal Arthur*, another of those deceptively named shore-training establishments. Philip found it a collection of dreary, tin-roofed huts behind the Wiltshire village of Corsham, ninety-eight miles from London.

Corsham was a school for petty officers and there were all told two hundred men there. But I think Philip felt it rather oppressive to be constantly preaching "Strands of discipline in each individual spring from confidence in authority, from loyalty and sense of duty, from anticipation of consequences pleasant and unpleasant . . ."

Life was not all beer and skittles at the Methuen Arms where he lived at Corsham, and Philip was like a boy out of school when he was invited to spend his first Christmas leave at Sandringham.

Uncle Bertie felt quite hard-hearted when he had to discuss the projected family tour to South Africa on the *Vanguard*, and explain that he couldn't permit Philip to come on board to bid Lilibet goodbye.

5

The visit to South Africa had been planned for more than a year both as a postwar spell in the sunshine for Uncle Bertie and his family and an opportunity for the King to see his youngest Dominion.

The Royal Family sailed on the *Vanguard* on February 1, 1947, and the new battleship was scarcely over the horizon when the Home Office admitted that arrangements for Philip's naturalization were in process.

The officials practically fell over themselves to explain that Philip would receive only the priority granted to all servicemen. And precisely six weeks later Lieutenant Philip Mountbatten formally took his oath of allegiance to King George VI.

Peter and I, living in Paris at that time, did not see the announcement in the London *Gazette* of March 18. It was just a formal entry in a list of over 800 naturalizations, showing that Philip had taken his mother's maiden name and was a British subject.

Nearly eighty years had passed since his grandfather, Prince Louis of Battenberg, had been similarly naturalized.

But I rather think that if Philip speculated on the figure of eighty years it was to compare it to the days of separation from Lilibet. Each day spent away now was a day of happiness denied.

He was impatient also with the sheer tedium of the Petty Officers' School. In the lecture room, to each new batch of students, he pointed to a chart, wand in hand:

DISCIPLINE

The force which causes a man to play the part required of him in the organization to which he belongs. It is:

A Guiding Force
An Inspiring Force
A Driving Force
A Controlling Force
A Comforting Force.

But Philip himself may well have found discipline singularly comfortless as the days lengthened and he still waited for his girl.

6

The Royal Family returned from South Africa in the middle of May and Lilibet's inner radiance as she stepped ashore was noticeable. We all knew that the past months' separation had been a dreadful strain. As the *Vanguard* steamed into harbor, in fact, Lilibet danced for sheer joy on the deck.

Philip was not in the family welcoming party at the Palace, but it was soon clear enough to everybody that she had spoken to him by telephone.

When Philip at last came up from Corsham, his first interview was with Uncle Bertie. Aunt Elizabeth had reminded the King a trifle sternly that Lilibet was now over twenty-one. Uncle Bertie took this admonition well. I believe that after talking to Philip he made some excuse about fetching photographs of the South African trip and slipped out of the room. When the door gently reopened, however, it was Lilibet.

Still nothing was said, but everybody in the family knew the truth as soon as they were seen walking in the Palace gardens with linked hands.

Formal requests had to be made to all the Dominion Governments, yet how secret is a secret? We soon all knew that on July 16 we should learn the great news officially. Pete and I had already discussed our wedding present.

In the meantime, the authorities were by no means lenient with Philip's leave from Corsham. His little green sports car came bustling through the traffic to park in the Palace court-yard on some days, but there were other days of disappointment when he could not come.

Sparklingly happy when they were together, he and Lilibet shared in the same restaurant parties as often as possible, at the Bagatelle, the Savoy and elsewhere, although they rarely danced.

There is an old story that one band leader, deciding to risk disfavor, struck up "People Will Say We're in Love" as soon as they entered the room, but Philip assures me this is sheer in-vention. Nevertheless, even to the public, the so-called secret was so open that people in the crowd at Lilibet's official appear-ances called out "Where's Philip?" much to her embarrassment.

In private, Philip fixed a sign, "Maggie's Playroom," on the door of the old nursery, to draw seventeen-year-old Margaret into all the gaiety of preparation, and I learned that he had even begun to re-arrange the Palace furniture.

The servants were a little uncertain how to treat this striding, energetic young man who had been a prince, was only now a naval lieutenant but obviously would soon be very much more.

Sometimes, I wondered what had really happened to Philip's temper. The full strength of it flashed out one day on a friend who had genially tried to joke, "You've chosen the wrong girl. Margaret is much better-looking!" Rage flared before Philip calmed himself to answer, "You wouldn't say that if you knew them. Elizabeth is sweet and kind, just like her mother."

Poor Philip was undoubtedly under severe tension during those few weeks. Once, walking down Bond Street, he hap-pened to gaze in a jeweler's window and then instantly turned away as he remembered the risks of an encounter with a camera-man and visualized the headline: "Philip Buys the Ring."

He decided, in fact, to ask his mother about the engagement ring, and a jeweler brought designs to Kensington Palace where Aunt Alice was staying. It was Philip's own idea that the ring should embody family sentiment, a large square diamond with smaller stones originally from a ring which Philip's father had given to Princess Alice. She studied the designs and then walked casually into the jeweler's fourth-floor office one afternoon, produced her own ring and asked for the stones to be recut and adapted to the new chosen setting.

As it turned out, it was the ring that timed events. As soon as he knew it was ready, on July 8, Philip rang up Lilibet and later spoke to Uncle Bertie.

That night, he went to the Palace for dinner but walked up to Lilibet's sitting room first. When they entered the dining room together, her right hand covered the fingers of her left hand. But Aunt Elizabeth at once went and kissed her.

"It's too big," Lilibet laughed, as she showed it to them. It was indeed, for though she had been shown a picture of the intended design, there had been no opportunity to try the ring on. "We don't have to wait till it's right, do we?" she then asked anxiously.

Uncle Bertie beamed and shook his head.

Thirty-six hours later all the world read the announcement:

Buckingham Palace, July 10, 1947
It is with the greatest pleasure that the King and Queen announce the betrothal of their dearly beloved daughter The Princess Elizabeth to Lieutenant Philip Mountbatten, R.N., son of the late Prince Andrew of Greece and Princess Andrew (Princess Alice of Battenberg), to which union The King has gladly given his consent.

Chapter 7

◆ The Wedding Story

1

WE HAD SCARCELY time next day to draft our message of congratulations before Peter picked up a London evening paper and
we saw that Philip had been instantly whisked into the midst of
the royal rigamarole, as we so often called the pomp and protocol
of royalty in our irreverent teens.

The very day after the engagement announcement, Lilibet
and Philip made their first appearance in public together at a
Buckingham Palace garden party. "They've wasted no time,"
said Peter. "It's rather like throwing him to the lions."

For the less experienced members of the Royal Family, these
traditional garden parties turn out to be not at all the pleasant
occasions they are painted.

Bishops and civil servants, servicemen and their wives, municipal do-gooders of every kind, the guests tend to arrange them-

selves into narrow avenues of staring eyes. Eventually one gets used to this human wall and discerns a line of smiles and friendly curiosity, but it takes time.

Philip must have been acutely aware of the critical eyes that examined him from within two yards or the inquisitive ears that strove to overhear every word as Lilibet proudly showed her engagement ring to her friends.

Hands clasped behind his back, bending forward protectively over his fiancée, he acquitted himself very well, so well that when the royal party reached their tea pavilion, the onlookers gave a cheer.

Uncle Bertie was so pleased that he did a comical little Charlie Chaplin dance. Just then, in that clowning indication of a cramp in his leg, the fates afforded a glimpse of the first of the ills that were to strike him down within five short years. But on that July afternoon of sunshine and showers the guests laughed and the portents remained unnoticed, the future unknown.

Within a week, Philip was launched on his first royal public duty when he had to accompany the Princess to see her invested with the freedom of the city of Edinburgh.

For the first time he had to watch his step, a step behind. He had to observe a string of new rules of public behavior, and yet appear relaxed.

When the Lord Provost demanded three cheers for the Princess, Philip joined in. When the National Anthem was sung, he sang with gusto. Afterward, as they drove together through the crowded streets, Scotland gave them a vociferous welcome and Philip had his first experience of the vibrating, deafening cheers, the ear-splitting tumult that was to greet him forever after.

That wonderful reception in Edinburgh transfigured the surge of unqualified approval and affection that flowed in from every part of the world.

The Monarchy had won unexpected prestige when it was realized that this was not a match of state but a marriage of two hearts.

Even viewing him with cousinly candor, I had to admit that Philip had all the charm and good looks one could wish for a prince. And he literally did not put a foot down wrong.

On that first evening in Edinburgh, the couple went to a public ball in their honor at the Assembly Room and danced the first dance, a double eightsome reel. With all its intricacies, Philip did it expertly with Lilibet and she could not conceal her surprise.

Deciding that reels were a certainty on the Edinburgh program, Philip had astutely rounded up Princess Margaret and the King's Piper beforehand and taken lessons.

This tiny detail pleased Uncle Bertie. "Philip is making out well," he said in a message to my Uncle Palo about the evening.

All the public engagements that could have crowded this period, nevertheless, had to be dovetailed with Philip's naval duties at Corsham.

When he returned to the Petty Officers' School he found that press photographers, with Admiralty permission, had even taken pictures of his iron bedstead and chest of drawers, still littered with pipes, family photographs and books.

All the newspapers, of course, were filled with stories of Philip, with numerous regal comparisons and flashbacks, even to the feckless Prince George of Denmark, who had come to England from the same Danish house of Oldenburgh and had fathered fourteen children for Queen Anne.

"I read about myself as if I were some animal in the zoo," Philip said. But as a bright idea to help his Corsham pupils develop habits of critical thinking, he had them cut out and study the widely differing tales told about him.

The slippings were pinned on the bulletin board with the caption, "Which paper do YOU read?" Philip himself read with amazement that he was bosom friends with the local butcher and undertaker and had demonstrated a gardener's skill by personally growing the school's prize-winning potatoes. It was true, of course, that he sometimes played skittles at the local pub, the Methuen Arms, and characteristically had organized the "locals" and the "Navy" into competing teams.

The skittle players heard the news of his engagement with awe and disbelief. "You must come to the wedding," Philip told them, and he made arrangements for many villagers to be on the groom's side in Westminster Abbey. During these months, he switched back and forth between the splendors of Buckingham Palace and the everyday life of the school and Corsham with great adroitness and ease. And his drives between one and the other were frequent.

But on one drive in his little green M.G., he took a different road, skidded at a corner and landed in a hedgerow. He was lucky to escape with bruises and a twisted knee. Already there was an immediate national outcry about his taking risks and jeopardizing the happiness of the Heiress Presumptive!

Almost in reply, he took Elizabeth, so long cloistered in Windsor, on trips with him. During the long summer evenings they would buzz out in the M.G. to Richmond Park and sit there like other young Londoners who found it a place to spoon. Lilibet wore a scarf over her head and Philip donned sunglasses, an effective disguise—one my husband and I employ to this day—that permitted them to travel unrecognized, though their pictures were everywhere.

In July, the King gave his formal approval to the marriage at a Privy Council meeting, and the question of where the young couple should live seemed settled when he presented them with a "grace and favor" mansion outside of Windsor Castle called Sunninghill Park.

This was one of those houses of the Crown secluded on hundreds of acres. The Army had knocked Sunninghill about during the war years and it needed extensive repair. Some resentment was aroused by the offer of even this dilapidated home because of the acute housing shortage in England at the time. The local authorities had been on the verge of taking over Sunninghill to convert it into workingmen's flats when the King's gift became known.

Talking it over, Philip and Lilibet realized that Sunninghill was a problem for other reasons. The place was not a palace. Part of the roof had been destroyed by fire during the war, and they could occupy only one wing. But, behaving like any engaged couple, they went to their new home often, strolling around the empty, echoing rooms and planning what it should be like.

Walking around the estate, they did not know, however, that their coming and going had been watched—by a workman perhaps from a nearby Army hut. One night, in August, the whole mansion, except for the service rooms, burned to the ground. Only the shell remained. The police acted quickly to discourage rumor and, to the public, ruled out the possibility of arson.

"How could it have happened?" Lilibet asked one of our friends confidentially. "Do you really think someone might have done it on purpose? I can't believe it." But, as they viewed the ruins, both she and Philip felt that however it had happened, it was probably for the best.

In the end, nothing marred the wedding mood. Girls jubilantly wrote to Lilibet to announce they planned to be married on the same day. The gifts began to pour in, too.

Philip found that he did not have to buy the wedding ring. That problem was solved when the people of Wales gave him a nugget of gold, a chunk so sizable that Lilibet said, "There is enough for two. We can save a piece for Margaret!"

This gift of Welsh gold struck Philip as a little impersonal. But he resolved his feeling by composing an inscription to be engraved on the inside of the ring, for his wife's eyes alone.

On the eve of the wedding, at a brief family ceremony at the Palace, Uncle Bertie touched his prospective son-in-law with a sword and created him Baron Greenwich, Earl of Merioneth and Duke of Edinburgh, and then invested him with the Most Noble Order of the Garter.

The first creation emphasized Philip's connection with London and with the sea; the second linked him with Wales. The third, the royal dukedom, was a most happy revival, for it had been previously borne by Queen Victoria's second son, the only British Prince elected by plebiscite King of Greece.

Uncle Bertie was always a stickler in these honors. Although he gave the Garter to Philip, he had already given it to Lilibet eight days before, in order to assure her seniority.

2

The wedding was beautifully organized. Soon after we accepted the formal invitation, Peter and I received a thick envelope by special envoy from the British Embassy in Paris. Inside were our travel tickets and detailed instructions as to which boat train to catch from Paris and how and where we would be met, and invitations to the State dinner and ball at Buckingham Palace, stipulating when Orders and decorations should be worn, and so forth.

Only Aunt Alice and one or two others were staying at Buckingham Palace. Claridges and other hotels were practically emptied to accommodate everyone else.

Our schedule asked us to arrive three full days before the wedding, and the Golden Arrow boat train that November night seemed almost a royal family special, for nearly everyone I met was a relative of mine.

At Victoria Station the Lord Chamberlain and other officials greeted us on the carpeted and decorated platform and we were driven straight to Claridges.

There we all found so many cousins, aunts and other kith and kin in the restaurant that we were constantly changing tables to talk to one another, in a whirl of amusing gossip. Among us were Auntie Sitta and Auntie Tim (the Queen of Romania and the Duchess of Aosta), the Comte de Paris, Queen Ena of Spain and our cousin, Michael of Romania, coming from behind the iron curtain to make his last visit abroad as reigning King.

I cannot remember who occupied the major royal suite but I rather think it was allotted to the King and Queen of Denmark. Precedent could have been a very delicate matter, except that none of us allowed it to worry him. Uncle Palo could not leave Greece and Freddie stayed at Buckingham Palace representing him as his Queen.

On the desks in our apartments there were formal schedules telling us the exact time we should leave Claridges to attend the State dinner (which proved to be a buffet) and what to do and what to wear at the wedding, complete with little seating plans.

Not that we all organized too thoroughly. Outside the hotel was the biggest line of rather old-fashioned limousines—"Queen

Mary" cars, as I called them—that I had ever seen. Peter and I used our own car and chauffeur, except for the wedding drive. There, as a modern convertible, it would have been out of place in the procession.

I did not see Philip before the wedding, but we privately knew he was getting "worked up," and no wonder!

How would you feel if you saw great grandstands erected along main avenues for your wedding?

Out of the mists of childhood, I remembered a young schoolboy confiding that he meant one day to have a good wedding, and now Philip was groom in undoubtedly the most exciting marriage of our day. At long last, the past—and the procedure—lay behind him.

The easiest thing of all, I think, was when he changed his religion (as George of Denmark had to do nearly two hundred fifty years before) by simply being "admitted into the Church of England," in a brief ceremony at Lambeth Palace conducted by the Archbishop of Canterbury. Philip had imagined complex oaths of renouncement but there was nothing of the kind. It is sometimes argued that he remains Greek Orthodox to this day, or since our church is in communion with the Church of England, that he need never have changed. But this is family chatter.

The day before the ceremony, Philip was so jittery that David Milford Haven, his best man, found that he had to exercise every ounce of tact and diplomacy to marshal him through the last bachelor rituals.

In reality, there were two final parties. The first one, to which the press was invited, ended at the Dorchester at 12:30. The second, with Uncle Dickie and David and a small select company, was held in private.

In the small hours Philip delivered his last formal words as a single man and was driven home to Kensington Palace. He did not cross the main processional route, where crowds were already bivouacking in the streets. And none of the people waiting by Kensington Palace that night even noticed the sleepy bachelor as he darted inside.

3

"Here they come!" I whispered to Peter. We had places of honor alongside the high altar, and the ranks in Westminster Abbey stretched away from us in blue and gold vistas.

We had been gathered in the forecourt of the Palace and driven to the Abbey in a procession of cars headed by Queen Mary and the Princess Royal.

The great masses of people behind the police and soldiers made a constant, unceasing pattern of color and sound. Hearing those cheers, moved by that wave of rejoicing, it was like sharing a little of one's own wedding and I took Peter's hand, thinking, "This is a welcome for us as well."

I gently took Peter's hand again as my cousin Philip came up the aisle with David. Here were the two boys with whom I had shared so much of my youth.

Philip didn't seem to have a cold as some say he did; he looked composed and dignified. I couldn't help thinking just a little of the past. I thought of him sick in his top hat at the funeral; I thought of the houses he had traced on the sand. Now the fanfare told him that his bride was approaching, and he looked toward Aunt Elizabeth and gave her his warmest smile.

One wanted to cry at this wedding. The age-old ritual caught at the heart. One noticed that Lilibet promised to love, honor and obey; one noticed that Aunt May (Queen Mary) dabbed her eyes. Perhaps the most sentimental moment of all came as the long bridal procession began to leave the Abbey.

As she was about to pass her parents, Lilibet turned and sank into a curtsey, first to her father and mother and then to Aunt May. The lovely folds of her wedding gown shimmered about her. Philip also half-bowed, holding her hand.

One could see that Uncle Bertie and Aunt Elizabeth had not expected such a gesture. One could see the muscle in Uncle Bertie's cheek working as it always did when he was deeply stirred. Then they bowed in return and Philip led forth his bride to the jubilant crowds.

The cheers lifted and almost intoxicated us as we ourselves drove to the Palace. We were all so gay and excited that, when Lilibet and Philip left to appear on the balcony before the people, we were in utmost confusion in the State rooms behind them.

A friend who was cheering with the crowds in the Mall imagined that we had formed a line, perhaps on the circling State staircase, waiting to be received. Not a bit of it. Most of us were even unaware that the bride and bridegroom were out on the balcony. We all moved back and forth, exclaiming, "Oh, I'm famished!" "I'm so thirsty!" "Thank goodness that's over!" "Oh, those chilly carriages!" or "Where's the loo?" And a stream of superbly gowned women disappeared in one direction and a stream of brilliantly uniformed men vanished in the other.

There was, in fact, no formal reception line to compliment the happy pair.

We found the State dining room bedecked with flowers. The famous gold plate was marshaled in full array, but, of course, it was the tiered wedding cake that caught our eyes.

I know that nine cakes were in fact made for the wedding,

though there was only this one at the reception itself. The others were cut up into hundreds of pieces and mailed, each in a white cardboard box with the silver initials "E-P," and people must have been sleeping on wedding cake for weeks afterward.

At the reception we sat six or eight to a table, and I found myself between Prince Bernhard of the Netherlands and David. "We were so nearly late!" he told me. "We overslept. And I had to have a cigarette—and had to go out and buy some. That wasn't all," he continued. "In the car we realized what an awful thing it would be if we accidentally exchanged caps. They looked identical—but mine would have fallen over Philip's ears. So we put an ink mark inside mine. It worked!"

We talked and laughed. "Filet de Sole Mountbatten, Perdreau en casserole and Bombe Glacée Princess Elizabeth" . . . I remember that I felt I couldn't wade through the menu, so I merely helped myself to the fruit in the middle of our table.

When we adjourned to the Blue Room for coffee, some who were interested in precedents were debating whose sword had cut the cake. There was, in fact, quite a mix-up in swords. It was reported that Philip, who did not have a sword for the wedding ceremony, had borrowed Uncle Dickie's.

Before the breakfast, Princess Margaret marshaled us for photographs, crying, "Come along, everybody!" and I remember that my husband borrowed David's sword for the picture, while Uncle Dickie, standing beside us, was wearing his own sword.

Ultimately it transpired that Philip's borrowed sword had belonged to his grandfather, Prince Louis of Battenberg. It was the one that the sailor prince had worn on his own wedding day, and thus all honors were satisfied.

I do hope Philip's alleged cold didn't continue to his honeymoon. Either he or Uncle Bertie had a sweet, considerate thought just before the going-away. The bridal pair were to drive through the chilly November evening in an open carriage, to let the people see them. Just beforehand, four hot-water bottles were put in, ready to be packed around Lilibet.

For millions and millions of people, this honeymoon was the apotheosis of twentieth-century romance, the honeymoon of all honeymoons, and it is amusing to think there were hot-water bottles, just in case.

Uncle Dickie had lent the newlyweds his country home, Broadlands, a satisfying and glamorous setting, though the house still bore the scars of its wartime use as a hospital.

We, in the family, properly forgot about the young couple as soon as we had peppered them with confetti and waved them goodbye; exhausted we returned to Claridges.

But the world continued to watch the honeymooners with morbid, almost frantic anxiety. It was a modern wedding equivalent, I think, of the prying old custom requiring members of a government to be present in the confinement room when the wife of a King gives birth to a child. (They even had to keep the door ajar at Claridges for the birth of my son Alexander.)

Thus cameramen converged on Broadlands, directed to spare no energy or expense in getting photographs. At a bend of the road where the house could be seen in the distance, crowds waited for hours for a long-range glimpse of the Princess and the Duke.

Police reinforcements, especially drafted, were deployed in the park to deal with trespassers. For people tried to hide behind trees or in the long grass. Randall, the Broadlands butler, felt it a personal slight, I think, when detectives searched even the chifforobes of the honeymoon suite.

When the couple went to Sunday morning services at Romsey Abbey, someone carried a sideboard into the churchyard to stand on to see over the crowd.

Philip derived some satisfaction from taking his bride out for an afternoon drive, flashing down the road at such speed that no one managed to do more than glimpse them, and outdistancing any pursuers.

Ultimately they both consented to take a short walk for the benefit of photographers but they made it pretty clear that that was all.

After a week, in fact, they went back to London and Philip's gentle irony could be detected in the message they issued, "The loving interest shown by our fellow-countrymen and well-wishers [has] left an impression which will never grow faint. We can find no words to express what we feel but we can at least offer our grateful thanks. . . ."

The real honeymoon was later at Birkhall, one of the smaller royal houses near Balmoral, an unpretentious eighteenth-century manor house, where the warmhearted local Scottish folk had the very good sense to leave them alone. It was December and snow cloaked the same hills that had been the scene of their courtship. It was bitterly cold, but Philip and Lilibet did not care.

Then, just before Christmas, they returned to Buckingham Palace, where Lilibet's suite had been enlarged to form two comfortable rooms and a sitting room.

I did not imagine that the newlyweds could possibly acknowledge all their wedding gifts, but by the time David joined us at St. Moritz we had received a pleasant letter thanking us for our little contributions, a perpetual motion clock and a Fabergé box.

"At long, long last, anyway," said David, as we discussed all Philip's faults and virtues, "he's got a settled home."

My mind went back to the wedding day, when as Philip and Lilibet drove away I tried to cheer up Uncle Bertie, who was looking quite miserable. "Now Philip's got you and Aunt Elizabeth, as well as Lilibet," I said. "He *belongs* now."

"That's right, Sandra," said Uncle Bertie, suddenly smiling. "He does belong. You're so right! Come and have a drink!"

Chapter 8

◆ The Duke of Edinburgh

1

AT SANDRINGHAM in the New Year Philip had several serious but jocular discussions with Uncle Bertie on a subject necessarily uppermost in their minds, the problem of Philip's future.

This was my cousin's second visit to Sandringham, for he spent Christmas there in 1946 as his introduction to the round of country living and sport in the keen Norfolk air. Now he was the son of the house, learning to share Uncle Bertie's intense interest in the day-to-day details of the estates and improving his proficiency with the guns so rapidly that there was no longer any need for his father-in-law to chide him for aiming too low.

Resolute on continuing his naval career on his own, Philip

was aware of his dissociation from civilian life imposed by his eight years in the service.

He had also not had the benefit of his wife's methodical tutelage in constitutional history, and he sensed in Lilibet a knowledge of statecraft and public service far greater than his own.

While marking time, Philip was temporarily appointed to the Operations Division of the Admiralty. As its youngest member, he eagerly sought out duties, determined not to miss the smallest opportunity of enriching his experience.

Two months before his wedding, he had made a maiden speech at the Cheam tercentenary celebration. "We recent old boys were just young enough to go out to be killed. I was one of the lucky ones. . . ."

Unveiling the village war memorial at Corsham, he said, "It is wrong to accept that another war is inevitable. It is only by each one of us actively working for peace all the time that we can improve its chances. . . . We hold a sacred trust. . . ."

My cousin, I could see, was writing his own speeches. His working day at the Admiralty ran from nine till six and, whenever possible, he reserved his public engagements for the evening hours. An evening that happened to be free was often filled quite deliberately with an impromptu visit or inspection. But then came his opportunity to close the admitted gaps in his education in a way acceptable to Uncle Bertie's line of thought.

He was appointed to a staff course at the Royal Naval College, Greenwich, and so found himself for the first time, like many other delayed wartime graduates, in an atmosphere resembling that of a university. The staff course is attended by commanders and captains.

Besides lectures in history and the strategy of war, including advanced naval strategy in atomic warfare, the student there embarks on a chosen course of reading which includes civics and economics. Peter tells me that one is just as likely to be studying the American Constitution as reading the *Influence of Sea Power* or other classic naval texts.

Philip found he was in the company of men several years older than himself, but he was also the partner of another lieutenant, happily young Donald MacLeod who had been his roommate and fellow instructor at Corsham.

It is an astonishing fact but for three months of his early married life Philip actually "lived in" at Greenwich.

Oddly enough, too, he was equipped at this time with no better fortune than his naval pay, supplemented by a wife's allowance of 87s.6d. per week.

Uncle Bertie had, however, sent a message to Parliament "relying on the liberality and affection of his faithful Commons," and a selected committee discussed finances for several weeks. Many estimates were examined before the committee decided by thirteen votes to five that the Duke of Edinburgh should receive an annuity of £10,000 ($48,000) a year. One wonders whether the dissidents were more generous than the "ayes." The £10,000 contrasted with the £30,000 voted to Prince Albert (as husband of a reigning Queen) in very different economic circumstances more than a hundred years before.

In order not to impose a burden on his people when they were faced with grave economic difficulties, Uncle Bertie advanced £100,000 from savings on his Civil List. He did not want the annuities to his daughter and son-in-law to require any actual outlay from the country for a period of time.

In addition to her annuity of £15,000 ($62,000), Lilibet was to receive £25,000 ($120,000), both subject to heavy income taxes.

I must say that Philip's stock rose high in my estimation when I found that he was prepared to keep his house in order within this budget and curb expenditures without sacrificing an ounce of royal dignity.

In announcing these provisions, the committee made it known that they considered "the responsibilities falling on the Duke of Edinburgh, as consort of the heiress presumptive, will be at least as great as those falling on the younger sons of a Sovereign." To paraphrase my close friend Sir Winston Churchill, rarely had so much been understood by so few.

Meanwhile, the modernization of a permanent London residence proceeded at Clarence House, and Windlesham Moor, near Sunningdale, a white stuccoed modern house of five bedrooms, was leased to afford the newlyweds a weekend release in the country.

Fortunately, Parliament voted £50,000 for the renovation of Clarence House; even a nation in economic durress was unwilling to have its Heiress Presumptive and her husband housed indefinitely in three rooms at Buckingham Palace.

After the Princess and Philip made the move, Peter went to lunch with them and he found Clarence House a modern home of comfort, dignity and charm, although the green-and-white dining room was big enough to be an officer's mess, and the huge drawing room was foredoomed to the disuse of all State apartments in the present day.

When Lilibet and Philip had first walked around, gas-lighting served some of the rooms, central heating did not exist and the only bath was to be found in a bedroom alcove. Somber oak darkened the corridors and the service quarters belonged to a bygone age.

The Ministry of Works architects discovered that Philip studied their plans meticulously, combining a quick eye for faults with an extraordinary flair for constructive suggestions.

Lilibet, I think, had always taken furnishing and decoration for granted, something that was there, conveniently supplied by others. Philip found an intense satisfaction in planning this first home, blending into it the furnishing and fittings thoughtfully donated as wedding gifts by colonial and dominion governments, public and private corporations, the heads of foreign states and hundreds of others.

Canada supplied the white maple paneling of Philip's study; the people of Lancashire subscribed all the furnishings for another room; and the city of Glasgow gave the white sycamore wall construction—bookcases, built-in wardrobes and other wonders—of Philip's bedroom.

By the time Peter visited Clarence House, every problem had been solved. Philip's sitting room was hung with the wonderful Laszlo portraits of his mother and father and his grandfather—and beside his desk a panel opened to reveal a completely modern drawing table.

In the dining room, with its Chippendale furniture, the finely carved and gilded light brackets of George III design looked as if they had been adapted from period candle sconces. "We had them made." Philip smiled.

And the Princess said proudly of the apple-green walls, "To get the exact shade, I mixed the paint myself."

The portraits of George II and his family gazed sternly down on the dining table, yet in other rooms there were contemporary Paul Nash paintings as well as Bateman cartoons. In Lilibet's sitting room, modern Steuben glass matched perfectly the metal of a Georgian chandelier. Scores of details testified to the thoroughness and imagination of the master of the house.

2

While serving at Corsham, Philip had a £500,000 idea. He mulled it over, laid it aside and brought it into discussions with

Uncle Bertie until it assumed definite shape. It concerned the National Playing Fields Association. On evenings out from Greenwich Philip had visited boys' clubs in the poorer parts of London, invariably to be dismayed at their lack of open-air playing space. With his common sense, Uncle Bertie saw that presidency of this organization could help forge civic links for Philip throughout Britain's intricate national life.

The affairs of the N.P.F.A. were rusty after years of wartime slow motion. The Association was saddled with heavy mortgages, overdrafts and other liabilities. But Philip worked out his £500,000 fund to reinvigorate it, in all the tangible terms of publicity—films, speeches, broadcasts, posters and so forth. And he went at the job with the furious energy of a bull at a gate.

With Uncle Bertie's full approval, he met the Council and officers at an unprecedented luncheon party at Buckingham Palace. It was the first of many unorthodox luncheons, conferences and measures which Philip began to introduce.

When his Greenwich staff course was completed, Philip went to the Playing Fields offices as regularly as any young man pursuing a business interest. He put in a full working morning, reserving the afternoon for other, rapidly developing public engagements.

It has been said that, as Duke of Edinburgh, Philip worked harder for the Association than any member of the Royal Family has worked to promote a cause since the Prince Consort, Albert, battled for the Great Exhibition.

In four years, under Philip's driving enthusiasm, the fund paid out £150,000 for some four hundred playing fields and had £350,000 available for future development.

Philip behaved rather like the chairman of an up-and-coming corporation. And as the plant got into operation new playing fields and children's playgrounds began building at the rate of two hundred fifty a year.

Princess Alice of Greece with her son, Prince Philip, the future Duke of Edinburgh.

Pix Inc.

Philip, age eight, rides with his cousin, King Michael of Romania, on a beach by the Black Sea.

Reuter Photo

Philip seated in class (*in front of Lawrence Sperry*) at the Mac-Jannet American School, at St. Cloud outside Paris.

Wide World Photos

United Press International

Philip (*second from left*) and his classmates practice archery.

The bride and bridegroom at Buckingham Palace after the ceremony.

The crowned heads of Europe assemble in Buckingham Palace after the wedding. Front row *(starting with third person, left to right)*: Princess Margaret; the Marquis of Milford Haven, best man; Princess Elizabeth; Prince Philip, Duke of Edinburgh; Princess Alexandra; King George VI; Queen Elizabeth; the Duke of Gloucester, with his son, Richard, standing before him; the Duchess of Gloucester; and *(at extreme right)* Crown Prince Gustav Adolf of Sweden; second row *(left to right, starting with third person)*: Countess Mountbatten; the Duchess of Kent; Princess Juliana of The Netherlands; Princess Andrew of Greece; Queen Mary; Queen Ena of Spain; Queen Ingrid of Denmark; Queen Frederika of Norway. In back row, only the men are identified: *(left to right)* Former King Peter of Yugoslavia; Earl Mountbatten; Prince Bernhard of The Netherlands *(his head half hidden)*; King Haakon of Norway; Prince George of Greece; unidentified man; King Frederik of Denmark; and King Mihail of Romania. The pages on either side of bride and groom are Prince Michael of Kent *(left)* and Prince William of Gloucester.

Photo from European

The royal couple acknowledges the cheers of the crowd from the balcony of Buckingham Palace.

On their honeymoon at Broadlands.

Photo from European

Philip working at his new naval duties, a staff assignment to the Royal Naval College.

British Information Service

The Coronation at Westminster Abbey, June 2, 1953. Philip supervised all the ceremonial arrangements as President of the Coronation Committee.

As the crowd roars, "God Save the Queen," the royal family appears on the balcony of the Palace after the Coronation.

Their attention is distracted momentarily as a group of jet planes flies over.

Philip smiles as the Queen Mother and Prince Charles ask Princess Anne a question.

After the trooping of the colors ceremony, Philip and the Queen "take the salute" of the Horse Guards in London, June 1953. He is exercising the special duties of his new position as Prince Consort.

With Prime Minister Sir Winston Churchill (*left*) and U. S. General Alfred Gruenther, Supreme Commander of NATO, at a dinner in London, June 1954.

Philip and Elizabeth relaxed their heavy schedule during 1955. Here they play with Prince Charles and Princess Anne at Balmoral Castle.

The royal family tours Scotland's Isles aboard their yacht, *Britannia*.

Arriving at Stockholm for a state visit to Sweden in June 1956, the royal couple is met by King Gustav Adolf VI and Queen Louise.

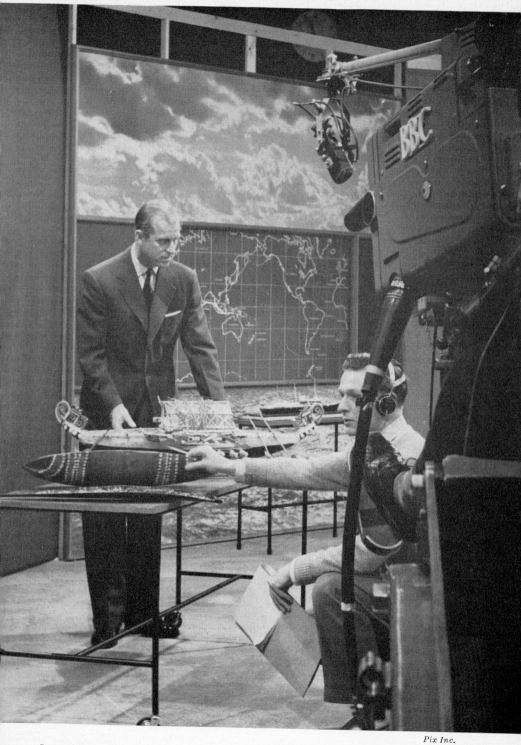

Pix Inc.

Learning to be a television personality, Philip checks an Australian native carrier he plans to show during a BBC broadcast of his world tour.

Assessing the field during a polo match at Cowdray Park, July 1957.

Pix Inc.

Accepting the gold cup from Lady Cowdray after his team won.

Pix Inc.

Returning hospitality, Philip and the Queen accompany President Eisenhower on a tour of Balmoral Castle with Princess Anne, October 1959.

A reunion with Earl and Countess Mountbatten in London, October 1959.

The royal family, with its newest member, Prince Andrew, March 1960.

"I'll go almost everywhere to open a new playing field," Philip once promised. He flew to Lerwick, in the Shetlands, to Manchester and Glasgow and the Midlands until the big map behind his desk at the N.P.F.A. was studded with flags denoting new recreation sites.

At a luncheon party, I remember a courtier of the old school was indignant because Philip had dined with a group of London publicans to help push a playing field. There were delightful old dears who feared that he might be going too far when he was photographed at a nightclub with newly divorced Frank Sinatra. The answer was that Sinatra donated the royalties of two of his best-selling records to the appeal and generously flew to London at his own expense to give an eight-minute performance when the Duke sponsored postwar London's first midnight theater show. The photographs to publicize the campaign helped the show which, that night, brought in £14,000 for the fund.

To accept a check for half that figure, Philip turned up at a reunion of the Butlin holiday campers at the Royal Albert Hall. For another appeal check, he went to Skegness and endured the gaze of five thousand bright-eyed girl campers singing "All the Nice Girls Love a Sailor." When he made a film, I marveled at his outward calm. "You think he was calm, ma'am?" one of the directors commented to me afterward. "That's why we sat him at a desk. His left leg was jumping with nerves."

Ultimately, of course, Philip costarred with Bob Hope in a fund-raising movie. It was about some boys trying to play cricket in a slum street and being chased by a bobby, until in desperation they wrote a letter about their problem to the Duke at Buckingham Palace. This picture was so successful that it netted £84,000 from a sympathetic public.

A plan to admit the public to the grounds of Buckingham Palace to watch a N.P.F.A. cricket match was never actually in prospect. But, on the other hand, Philip regularly played in fund cricket matches at Arundel Castle, and it was decided that a boxing tournament promoter could legitimately be invited to the Palace to hand over a cheque. He arrived correctly wearing his N.P.F.A. green-striped tie.

Philip never refused an engagement. He would try to fit it into his appointment book. A typical day in Edinburgh was scheduled for a Scottish playing fields committee. Before it was over, he had inspected three guards of honor, walked in procession to church with the magistrates, lunched with the Lord Provost, visited a local mariners' club, taken an Army salute, watched a fly past and been vociferously cheered through the city.

Packed into a few exciting months, the appeal gave Philip his first general experience in public speaking. He was indeed like a young man in a big business organization being primed as a higher executive. For Philip, however, the business was a nation and the firm was the Royal Family.

3

In addition to N.P.F.A. affairs and a course of spare-time naval study as an aftermath to Greenwich, the momentum of activities quickened continually for Prince Philip during 1948 and 1949.

These were his important years of initiation as a collateral figure of the monarchy and within six months his cheerful diligence had brought him tremendous public approval.

A notable landmark was a visit to Paris in May 1948, to open an exhibition of eight centuries of British life.

This afforded Lilibet a first journey to a foreign country.

Philip found it in striking contrast to his quiet visit to Monte Carlo as Lieutenant Mountbatten the previous year.

What was to be a semiprivate trip to the French capital nearly assumed the proportions of a full State visit; behind the scenes, as it turned out, Philip underwent a trying test of the disciplines to which kings and queens, princesses and consorts, are subject in the twentieth century.

We had received the delightful news of the family event that Lilibet expected for the late fall and knew Philip was solicitous of the strain that Paris might cause. Lilibet, pale, took it all with immense self-control: the visit to the President, the laying of the wreath at the Arc de Triomphe, the drive to the Opéra, and everywhere the wonderful welcome of the people.

But on the Sunday when they were due to attend morning services at the British Embassy Church, history repeated itself: Philip found himself feeling as sick as he had felt at the funeral service in Athens; he looked green. Lilibet wanted to cancel his engagements for the rest of the day but he would not allow her to. He insisted on going to church and taking communion.

In the afternoon, after he had been thoroughly sick, he went to the races at Longchamps and put on an actor's exhibition of good spirits not to disappoint the French crowds.

That night the British Embassy took over a nightclub in honor of the Duke and the Princess, with admission formally limited to official guests. It was a dull and discreet show, yet when Philip and Lilibet returned to London, they learned that an English clergyman had fulminated about "a dark day in our history."

The public knew nothing of Philip's illness or how he had ignored it earlier. The clergyman's attack underlined the maxim that one cannot please all the people all the time, and Philip rightly paid no attention to such criticism.

So he dealt with later "incidents," even at home.

When receiving the Freedom of Edinburgh, he made a speech in his happiest mood referring to a former dinner with the Lord Provost. "He very kindly offered us one for the road. When somebody said the train was twenty minutes late, we had another. . . . We eventually decided that the train was six drinks late."

In cold print this good humor offended certain circles and provided ammunition for the old school who believed that royal speeches should be written in formal terms and read with equal formality. Philip, however, refused to conform. He was responsive rather to the new breezes in the nation—that did take it in the proper spirit.

On one occasion, the comptroller of the "Clarence household," Sir Frederic Browning, actually wrote a speech for Philip. At the banquet at which it was to be delivered, this genial ghost listened expectantly to see how his words would sound. Prince Philip pulled out his notes, put them aside and then began an entirely different speech—and a very successful one—in his own words.

General Browning was never asked to write another speech. Always prepared to speak wittily off the cuff, never at a loss for a phrase, Philip was soon being hailed as the best after-dinner speaker in London. And on the two- or three-day tours with Princess Elizabeth to Lancashire, to Northern Ireland, to the Midlands and elsewhere, some of my more watchful relatives noted that he was being welcomed in his own right. However undefined his duties, however secondary his status, he had secured the recognition that he was not merely a glorified courtier, not a husbandly cipher, and that his position as second was strictly relative.

At a big civic ceremony in which he was admitted to the Freedom of the City of London and made his first speech at the Guildhall, he exemplified the Philip touch when he modestly asserted that he accepted the Freedom for the millions in the Second World War who had contributed to the peace. "The ideal that my wife and I have set before us," he told the Lord Mayor and the guests, "is to make the utmost of the special opportunities we have to try to bring home to our own generation the full importance of that contribution."

By his twenty-seventh birthday, Philip was appointed a personal aide-de-camp to King George VI. With his sense of occasion, Uncle Bertie saw that Philip's first official function in that post was to meet his Uncle Dickie at London Airport, when he returned from India as Viceroy.

4

Just as Uncle Andrea had loved Mon Repos, Philip, as a young husband, loved his weekends at Windlesham. It was the first house he could call his own.

He enjoyed being alone there with his wife, especially during the happy summer they awaited the birth of Charles. He had escaped from Buckingham Palace which, from Windlesham, looked like a stuffy de luxe hotel.

He enjoyed the morning drives to Windsor Great Park for walking or riding and the congenial afternoon visits to his in-laws at Royal Ledge. He liked inviting his own friends for the weekend, bringing his wife into contact with a wider world than she had known before. He would talk of past, present and future, bent on sharing with Lilibet his own broad knowledge of places and people.

He was no longer the hungry old Philip I knew; he was trimming down, watching his diet with evident concern. This was quite absurd; the men of our family have been of the lean kind as long as we can remember. But when Lilibet ate a full English breakfast, Philip contented himself with coffee and toast. When she nibbled sandwiches at afternoon tea, Philip took only tea without sugar. And·always on the weekends he would unleash his extrovert energy in furious exercise.

It is sometimes said that the one game Philip has never played is golf; yet Windlesham had a small course and he borrowed clubs to try it out. Cricket, especially, struck responsive chords in everything he liked about the English way of life. Inside of a few weeks at Windlesham he adapted the soft tennis court to a cricket pitch and mobilized friends, chauffeurs, detectives and gardeners into a team to play against other local squads.

When a match was not in the offing, Philip practiced batting or bowling with a secretary or chauffeur. And when he could find no partners in gamesmanship, he would don three or four sweaters to run around the grounds. "Really, I am sure Prince Philip is mad," Lilibet said laughingly one day.

At Buckingham Palace, Philip revived the old squash court and he often used the swimming pool. He was there with Michael Parker, batting a ball about and plunging into the pool, the night Prince Charles was born.

The birth of Charles was a great royal event; he was the first child born in direct line of succession in more than fifty years. The 7-pound, 6-ounce prince was King George VI's first grandson. Through both his parents he was the fortieth generation in descent from Alfred the Great.

His arrival found a welcoming crowd of thousands pressed against the Palace gates. Yet Philip went to Lilibet's side in just a shirt and flannels—the way Peter had come to me the night Alexander was born (on July 17, 1945), and oddly enough, at

9:14, precisely the same hour and minute. The casual dress seems, in retrospect, all part of the unconventional, easier new deal for royalty.

Uncle George (Prince George of Greece) flew from Paris to represent my family at the baptism and was one of Charles's godparents.

The little Prince was christened Charles Philip Arthur George. His last two names were the last names of Uncle Bertie, but they were also given for the fondly remembered Uncle George Milford Haven whose widow was a godmother, and for our Uncle George himself, who had helped equally to inspire Philip's lasting passion for the sea.

5

For a time, shortly before the birth of Prince Charles, Philip had been so deeply involved in public duties that his naval career seemed to be in jeopardy. Uncle Bertie's failing health caused many responsibilities to devolve on Philip as his unofficial deputy. A tour of Australia and New Zealand was planned for Uncle Bertie and Queen Elizabeth in 1949 and this in turn suggested an even greater increase in engagements for their son-in-law at home.

Reluctantly facing this reality, Philip worked it out with the Admiralty authorities to go on half-pay. This arrangement left him free to resume full naval duties at some time in the future when less pressed.

Lilibet's temporary retirement also meant new demands on Philip. Regiments were still to be reviewed, memorials unveiled, factories visited and the calendar of traditional functions had to be carried on.

It was symptomatic that just at this time he parted at last with his little M.G. in favor of a big, fast Austin Sheerline and—for public functions—a specially built Rolls Royce, with much of the equipment fitted to his own plans.

When Lilibet took up her duties again, each month brought a two-day tour of the provinces, with the formality of stately arrivals in a royal train and, of course, the endless round of inspections, the signing of vellum civic parchments with golden pens, and foundation-stone laying, a ceremony Philip always thought rather futile.

The Duke would smile through the little contretemps that occurred, but they never found a chink in Lilibet's confidence: she always knew·exactly what to say and what to do.

Throughout these months, Philip was rapidly acquiring a knowledge of ceremonial usages, a fuller sense of the Crown as a living institution and there arose in him too a deep urge to keep the monarchial system working smoothly in a world in which traditions were constantly being scrapped.

There were journeys to the West Country, to Yorkshire, to the Channel Islands on the training battleship *Anson*, and, whenever they were home, the young couple used to try to find time to go over to Clarence House to see how the improvements were getting on.

When the house was nearly ready, Philip typically took off his coat to help the men arrange the furniture. He knew precisely where he wanted it placed. Typically, too, the day they moved in, in July 1949, the Duke had a playing fields meeting in Wiltshire and could not join Lilibet in the new home until the evening.

Peter and I had just gone to Venice to stay with Mummie, and at the news of the move, he commented, "History repeats itself. Fifty years ago, my great-grandfather, the *other* Duke of Edinburgh, used to live there."

I was able to tell my husband that modern events had supplied a closer, though more trivial link between our families. When we were in London, we had a Swedish cook, Mrs. McKee, who had naturally been closely vetted by the Special Branch of Scotland Yard.

Lilibet and Philip's comptroller were looking around for a cook, found that Mrs. McKee was available and took her on to Clarence House. As Mummie had once had Uncle Andrea's cook, so Philip now had ours.

The way it happened, Philip did not have much time to enjoy her cooking: we soon had news that, after all, he would be going to sea again.

Although the doctors had decided that Uncle Bertie's proposed tour of Australia could not take place, his health had improved so much that there was no reason for not allowing Philip to devote full time to the Navy. It was stressed that he should resume his naval duties without publicity, and he was assigned to the destroyer flotilla leader *Chequers* with the Mediterranean Fleet.

Once aboard, he tacitly dropped the title of Duke of Edinburgh. To his South African captain, Jack McBeath, he became "Number One," the usual term for first lieutenant.

Uncle Dickie Mountbatten, who had met Philip at Malta Airport, had tactfully explained that he was there "as uncle, not as admiral"; as soon as Philip had climbed the gangplank of the *Chequers* the cameramen and the reporters had had no chance. Thus, after his strenuous two years in the public eye, my cousin switched suddenly from the splendor of Clarence House to the cabin of a "Jimmy the One," stuffy and cramped, plumbing pipes coiling above the bunk, which was his first love.

Chapter 9

◆ Interlude in Malta

1

IN THE SUMMER of 1950, after he had been on duty in the Mediterranean nine months, Philip entertained Uncle Palo and Freddie (King Paul and Queen Frederika of Greece) aboard the *Chequers*. Then, in the late fall, he and Lilibet paid a visit to Palo and Freddie at home in Athens, and so eventually I heard a good deal of my cousin's last active days in the Navy, a phase of his life that is curiously little known.

Behind Philip's great desire to resume his naval career, there was an ulterior motive, but I hasten to add that it was completely unselfish.

Philip was a man who had frequently enjoyed the commonplace side of life before making a spectacular marriage, and now he wanted his wife to experience the pleasures of a more ordinary existence as he had done. To a large extent he succeeded in this aim. Instead of the unchanging routine of December at Sandringham, Lilibet flew out to join him at Malta for their second wedding anniversary and was with him until just after Christmas. The ship was refitting in the dockyard, giving Philip plenty of time ashore.

The Edinburghs, as they were soon known on the island, stayed with the Mountbattens at the Villa Guardamangia at Pieta, a largish house which Uncle Dickie had rented. Here their lives were not very different from any other naval couple. Seven of the fourteen officers on board the *Chequers* had their wives in Malta, and Lilibet enjoyed playing her part in the unaccustomed round of entertaining this youthful social group.

Philip found, nevertheless, that her position as Heiress Apparent could never be ignored. The Governor's Ball was given in her honor. Dutiful visits were paid, at her own suggestion, to hospitals and schools. Lilibet, as usual, could not go shopping without drawing a crowd and her personal detective accompanied her whenever she went out with the car.

But it did make a difference to be leading a life in new surroundings. Official mail from London was drastically curtailed and, like any other naval officer's wife, Lilibet waved goodbye to her husband early every morning and then took her time in embarking on the pleasant program of the day.

Philip played polo in the afternoons if he were free, and the Princess would sit watching with other officers' wives. In the evening the royal couple went dining and dancing at the Phoenicia, the local hotel, or sometimes took a launch to the neighboring creeks and bays around Malta and Goza. And Uncle Dickie would give a children's party where Philip and Lilibet manned the swings and slides.

Philip relished these pleasures outside official routine but also enjoyed being back in naval harness. He was responsible for the discipline, stores, welfare and operation of his destroyer. He soon had a reputation for being strict but not as a martinet. The *Chequers* had a string of sporting trophies which Philip made sure they kept.

He put in spare time work maintaining the interests he had developed in Britain, even to making a five-minute film about one of the local islands, to be used at home as part of an appeal for national playing field funds. And he took a lively concern in the Buckingham Palace catering campaign about which he wrote to Uncle Bertie to keep *au courant*.

On her first Malta visit, Lilibet remained until two days after Christmas. Before she left for Britain, the *Chequers* had been assigned to routine patrols in the Red Sea. In April, Lilibet returned to the island to celebrate her twenty-fourth birthday with Philip. A gala party was held at the Villa.

These were especially happy days for both of them. Off duty, Philip drove Lilibet all over Malta, exploring landmarks, making plans for the new baby known to be on the way and for Prince Charles.

At twenty-nine, in July, he was promoted to the rank of lieutenant commander, in the ordinary way, having completed eight years as a lieutenant. With the promotion came his first active naval command: the frigate *Magpie*.

But Philip did not finish his assignment on the *Chequers* before he made an official four-day visit to President Camille Chamoun of Syria, during which, I have heard it said, there was an attempt on his life. I never have had confirmed all the details but there were press reports that an assassin was brought to trial, charged with trying to blow up a store in Damascus while the Prince was in it. On the other hand, Philip says it was just a rumor.

Soon he received home leave that happily coincided with the birth of Princess Anne at Clarence House. "It's the sweetest girl," he said on the telephone to his grandmother at Kensington Palace. The news went at once to Princess Alice, who was staying there.

2

When Philip was ceremoniously piped aboard H.M. Frigate *Magpie* in September 1950, he found the crew of one hundred eighty-six drawn up in divisions on a compact, armament-loaded ship.

The old seadog of our family, Uncle George, took a particular interest in this new assignment. It was George, I believe, who explained that the *Magpie* was a sister of the famous *Amethyst*, which had defied Chinese Communist guns on the Yangtze, and that she was a former U-boat hunter, as dashing a little frigate as any in the Navy.

Addressing his men, Philip said he meant to make the *Magpie* live up to her looks. "It will be up to you," he concluded, "and up to me." It could have been Uncle Dickie speaking. It was another occasion on which a Mountbatten had set out to make his ship the finest afloat.

The *Magpie* already held several naval records and Philip, inevitably, determined to add the laurels of sport. He succeeded, for his crew won six out of ten events in a forthcoming regatta.

I am told he practiced the crews until their hands were blistered, and that he stroked one shell himself.

In October, he flew home for Anne's christening at Buckingham Palace. Among the godparents were Aunt Alice and Princess Margarita, his sister. And he supplied a typical touch: he took with him his Maltese steward, Vincent, had him watch the baby baptized, and afterward introduced him to Uncle Bertie. The gesture, which endeared Philip to the whole island of Malta, is still remembered.

When my Uncle Palo visited Philip aboard the *Magpie*, there was nowhere to entertain a King of Greece but the wardroom. Here Palo found with astonishment that Philip was simultaneously carrying on a lot of his English office work, including the preparations for the Festival of Britain and plans for an overseas tour.

There was no room on board ship for a secretary, and no officer who could be delegated to the duty. Uncle Palo was under the impression that Philip had at least a dictaphone, but the rough reality was that he spent hours drafting his own letters and memos in pencil.

He also imagined, I think, that he would find a qualified commander acting as nominal first lieutenant under Prince Philip— but again nothing of the kind. My cousin was junior to all other ship captains in the flotilla.

But the *Magpie* in time became the "cock ship." On one occasion, I believe, her royal skipper won praise for his skill in taking the frigate out of the tricky shallows of Monte Carlo harbor during a squall, though I gather that the senior officer of the fleet had waited for the wind to subside before venturing to do it himself.

I do not know how Philip found time for his water skiing,

polo and other sports. For example, he had not been in command three months when he had to blend naval and State duties by taking his ship to Gibraltar to open the new Legislative Council on behalf of the King.

On another cruise, he dined with King Ibn Saud of Saudi Arabia at Jeddah and was received by and dined with King Abdullah of Jordan in Amman.

He went to Cyprus, Algeria and, in Egypt, he found himself in Alexandria and Cairo where he had gaily sought to make the best of the bad job of war ten years earlier. He also revisited Venice where the irrepressible students of the University of Venice staged a mock trial in Latin, charging him with having fair hair and invading the Doges' domain. Replied Philip, with truth, "I am a descendant of the Vandals and the Goths and if it had not been for them there would not have been a settlement in Venice at all. . . . I merely came to see how it was getting along."

Lilibet now flew to Malta as often as possible. Uncle Dickie had left the island to become Fourth Sea Lord, so the Edinburghs leased the Villa Guardamangia themselves. They did it with an air of permanence when they brought in their own plate and linen as well as their own Daimler and Hillman cars.

Princess Margaret arrived there for a few days' visit, and Prince Bernhard of the Netherlands was entertained during Anglo-Dutch naval exercises. When the *Magpie* sailed on antisubmarine exercises, Lilibet had the other officers' wives for tea. She became fully primed on local gossip including the fact that her husband's shipboard nickname was "Dukie."

Then Lilibet began to join in the round of Mediterranean jaunts, which Philip was, in fact, largely responsible for planning.

They paid a week's visit to Uncle Palo and Aunt Frederika, the Princess' first trip to our native land. The frigate *Surprise*, which had been fitted out as the commander-in-chief's Mediterranean dispatch vessel, offered her suitable accommodation, and Lilibet sailed aboard this ship while the *Magpie* and a destroyer acted as her escorts. The voyage was lighthearted, typified by these early morning radio signals.

Surprise to *Magpie*: "Princess full of beans."

Magpie to *Surprise*: "Can't you give her something better for breakfast?"

Athens was decorated for Lilibet and Philip's arrival, and they had a wonderful welcome. I was in America at the time or I should dearly have loved to share the occasion.

Every young man likes to return with his wife to the places where he enjoyed happiness before the felicity of marriage, and I like to think of Philip showing Lilibet the hundred steps that led to Mummie's house and the quiet house—now overshadowed by apartment blocks—where Aunt Alice used to delight him and dismay me with orange compote.

3

The Duke of Edinburgh's command of the *Magpie* lasted from September 1950 until July 1951. The eleven months were terribly short, but filled with every kind of enjoyment, from the thrill of commanding his ship to the pleasures of travel with Lilibet to the fun of underwater fishing or explorations of the local islands.

An officer who was on the *Magpie* glows with warmth when he tells me how popular Philip was with his crew. He was fond of driving the skimmer, the frigate's fast motor launch. He would be piped to it with naval solemnity but then take the wheel unceremoniously, assigning the coxswain to the back seat.

Philip had just the right touch, too, when he sent a portion of Anne's christening cake to the wives and families of each mess. It seemed that he couldn't go wrong when he represented the ship at the naval games in javelin throwing. I am afraid, in this event, that the *Magpie* did not win, in spite of a hefty throw executed with Gordonstoun technique.

Now the duties of the future closed in faster. Plans were afoot for a trans-Canadian tour with Lilibet in the autumn. Despite failing health, Uncle Bertie had refused to cancel the round-the-world tour to Australia and New Zealand the following year and it was becoming increasingly clear that Philip and Lilibet would go instead, as his deputies.

In creating his program for civilian life, Philip had accepted an offer to become President of the British Association for the Advancement of Science for the following year. This involved giving an inaugural address to the distinguished scientists in assembly but he was not deterred. A short ready-made address was offered to him. He declined it.

Although so much has been made of his temerity, he knew, as a matter of fact, that two other members of the Royal Family had felt fully equal to the task of making this talk. The Prince Consort had addressed the Association in 1859 and so had the Duke of Windsor, then Prince of Wales, in 1926. Philip's boldness lay in taking the role so seriously that he decided to deliver a full-dress speech that could stand as a contribution to science on its own.

He spent an hour or two every day aboard the *Magpie* for several weeks preparing it. With dozens of reference books sent from London, he read and assimilated, writing the first drafts on signal pads, and revising and editing the speech until the last word was nearly right.

Actually, he was never content with it. His brother officers found that he lived with the "words and music," so to speak, day and night, at sea and off watch. Finally he had a fifty-page review of a century's scientific progress, and when he saw the mass of typescript he still cut some five pages, leaving an address timed to last about an hour.

When Philip left the *Magpie*, his staff in Malta had never seen him so depressed. He is supposed to have made a farewell speech to the assembled crew, declaring, "The past seven months have been the happiest of my sailor life."

After the official three cheers, extra cheers for "Dukie" still rang over the water while a launch following him to the shore fired a "21-gun" salute of smoke flares.

Four days later, Philip flew to London. The plane landed briefly at Nice and, after the take-off, he looked down sadly at the coast until the villas and vineyards dropped out of sight. As the plane winged toward the mountains, he took out his British Association speech and studied it.

It was a more mature, restrained and authoritative young man altogether who returned from his naval tour. A month later the enormous success of his speech may have helped to compensate him for leaving.

The Assembly turned out to be one of the largest gatherings of scientists ever held in the British Isles. An audience of two ·thousand people packed the largest hall of Edinburgh University, and another two thousand followed the proceedings by special television.

Philip's confidence in delivering his opinions to the scientists has been compared with the audacity of a physicist who might address the Royal Family on the functions of monarchy. But his self-assurance carried conviction and his superb platform manner added gloss to his subject matter.

He opened blandly with the words, "Your kind invitation to

me to undertake the office of your President for the ensuing year could not but startle me on its first announcement. The high position which science occupies . . . contrasted strongly in my mind with the consciousness of my own insignificance . . ."

But just as the scientists were leaning back, warm and flattered, Philip revealed that he was merely quoting the words his great-great-grandfather, Prince Albert, had used, and his review swung forward to his own highly pertinent comments.

"The rate at which scientific knowledge is being applied in many industries is too small and too slow. . . . Scientific knowledge has reached a point where we can either set the world free from drudgery, fear, hunger, and pestilence, or obliterate life itself . . ."

Then, after an hour, he concluded.

"It's clearly our duty as citizens to see that science is used for the benefit of mankind. For of what use is science if man does not survive?"

The scientists applauded, the press waxed enthusiastic, the world responded with approval. Here was a challenging spokesman rising unexpectedly in royal circles.

Recuperating at Balmoral, Uncle Bertie noted Philip's success with great pleasure. He had read the speech beforehand and in fact suggested one small cut, dealing with the suppression of patents, which Philip had made without question. Like the discipline he had once preached at Corsham, Philip was becoming a guiding force, an inspiring force, a driving force.

GOD IS MY HELP

Chapter 10

◆ The Conquest of Canada

1

IN THE CALM months before the Canadian tour, Philip enjoyed occasional diversions such as sailing his yacht *Bluebottle* at Cowes. When he appeared in any afternoon race, boatloads of press photographers, eager to get a maximum view, annoyed him considerably. But fortunately there were evening hours when he could sail forth by himself from the peaceful Beaulieu River and skim the waves undisturbed.

During this soft autumn spell, he and Lilibet were still able to continue some of the pleasures which they had in their Malta sojourn, such as impromptu evenings out. In fact, they went dining at one London restaurant-nightclub no fewer than eight times.

Meanwhile, the plans for the Canadian trip were drafted and redrafted to perfection. Invitations from scores of Canadian institutions had accumulated. One day, a secretary and a government representative unrolled a huge map of Canada on the floor of Lilibet's sitting room at Clarence House and Lilibet and Philip crawled around on their hands and knees estimating distances and selecting stops. Ultimately, the tour, which had been planned for three cities and ten days, ballooned into a ten-thousand-mile odyssey to last thirty-five days. And, although we did not know it at the time, the trip was to become a searing test of the physical and emotional strength of both of them.

I doubt whether Lilibet and Philip ever faced a harder itinerary. By the time they had finished their holiday at Balmoral, it had been laid out to the last wreath-laying, the twenty-first signing of a golden book, the fiftieth mayor with whom they would have to shake hands.

Naturally, they agreed to practically everything proposed by their Canadian hosts, who, it must be said, were extremely enthusiastic. The days were lengthened into fourteen-hour schedules, and reception lines into thousands of hands.

Lilibet and Philip planned to leave England by sea on September 25 on the liner *Empress of France*. Four intercommunicating staterooms had been converted into a royal suite. Then, just a week before the departure, Uncle Bertie's doctors advised him he should undergo a lung operation.

The start was therefore delayed. But it could not be indefinitely postponed and, ultimately, Elizabeth and Philip made up time by flying in a B.O.A.C. airliner. They took off after midnight on October 8 and touched down at Dorval Airport, Montreal, at noon, Canadian time, the next day. The flight was dismal, however, because of their anxiety about Uncle Bertie's condition and the burden of keeping it absolutely secret.

Philip watched the dawn from the flight deck and wrote to one of his sisters afterward about the ecstasy of the view. Studying Captain O. P. Jones at the controls, he was seized with the desire to learn to fly, an ambition he fulfilled two years later. But, as they passed the long Atlantic trip, he was most attentive to Elizabeth.

When the Princess stepped down the gangway of the aircraft onto Canadian soil, Philip in fact knew what the crowds at the distant fringes of the airport did not know—that his wife was trembling with nerves. The real story behind that first Canadian tour was that she left a terribly family ordeal three thousand miles back and now faced a public ordeal ahead. And Philip also knew what had been concealed from Uncle Bertie himself: that the King's whole left lung had been removed for cancer.

Though Philip was outwardly composed, he was terribly worried. So serious were the hazards facing the King that Elizabeth carried in her dispatch case a sealed envelope containing a draft accession declaration and a message to the British Parliament. The envelopes were to be opened in the event of Uncle Bertie's death, and only Philip was aware of their existence.

But, as the immense program got under way, the news from home was happily reassuring. The welcome of the crowds, awed and silent at first, grew to frantic, uninhibited enthusiasm by the time they reached Toronto.

Thousands of students chanted, "Betty Windsor, Rah, Rah, Rah" while groups of girls everywhere called, "Phil, Phil, Phil!" Quick to make wisecracks, Philip continuously kept the Princess smiling. "We've seen that woman before," he would say, as they rolled past another multicolored line of wildly yelling Canadians. "I recognize her by her teeth!"

The news of the tour could often be heard by radio in the royal car, and Philip devised a game of locating the commentator. It ranked high points if they could spot the man with the microphone and hear his excited voice change in pitch, "I believe the Princess just waved at me!"

As the miles went by, the sheer multiplicity of the incidents of welcome could have created a bemusing, drugging effect, but Philip was so attentive that hardened reporters were impressed. Once, when a child threw a bouquet at the car, Philip did miss the gesture, and it was Elizabeth who drew his attention in time to acknowledge it. But such was the partnership between the two that, when Philip saw a boy photographing the Princess, vainly trying to get her in focus, he, in turn, strolled over and waved aside officials and others in the way of the camera.

I know how difficult it is to reciprocate the enthusiasm of a crowd, how difficult a royal task at a reception to give a smile or an acknowledgment to everyone. Philip was magnificent in his constant support of his wife. In a receiving line, he would frequently detain the next person due to shake her hand by engaging him or her in conversation. This allowed Elizabeth a needed respite. Though, at receptions, it was their habit to separate to talk to different groups of people, he always moved protectively toward her if a crowd began to press.

In one city, the Mayor had made plans for a luncheon at which they would be seated under a spotlight for the view of the thousand-odd guests. Elizabeth would have accepted the plan without complaint. But Philip thought it would be too grueling and he made no bones about it, so it was arranged for them to lunch privately.

A Canadian summed it up when he said that Philip worked and made arrangements constantly to assure the tour's success. The Governor General of Canada had the idea that Elizabeth and Philip should join in a square dance at Ottawa's Government House, garbed in the checked shirts and dungarees the occasion required. When, afterward, they went to the railroad station still in costume, much to the delight of onlookers, Philip himself insisted on driving the royal train on to Hamilton. At a small way station on the route, five families waiting to see the train go through were astounded when it stopped and backed up to them. Philip saw to it that Elizabeth came out on the rear platform for a few moments to chat.

Intensively reported by press and radio each day, these spontaneous touches won Canadian hearts. But Philip's best brainwave, I think, was when he suggested a clear plastic top to the royal car so that Lilibet could be seen perfectly in any kind of weather. An aircraft plant worked without a break to manufacture three such tops and the first was ready in time for a rainstorm in Winnipeg.

"How do I look?" the Princess asked over the intercom.

"Like an orchid wrapped in cellophane," Michael Parker, Philip's secretary, complimented her gaily.

The Princess' spirits lifted as the news from Buckingham Palace improved, but there were moments when Philip could not help showing how much he felt the entire strain.

The newspapers had gone all out to give the tour what they called complete coverage, but he quickly resented some of their actions.

In Toronto, when he found cameramen obstructing the view of a group of school children, he indignantly stood up in his car to wave them to one side. "What are they belly-aching about now?" he growled, after Lilibet and he had posed for pictures at Niagara where the news photographers still wanted more.

At a reception for Canadian newspapermen who were not coming on to the United States with them, he observed suddenly that the Princess and he were shaking hands with some correspondents who were in fact remaining with the party and who had simply gate-crashed. "This is a waste of time," he declared, turning on his heel and walking away.

At the same time, Philip exerted all his patience, stamina and knowledge to keep the great tour a triumph. It was not enough to create his own improvements and protect and support Lilibet in every way. The night before addressing an assembly of Toronto businessmen, for his one speech on the trip, he sat up till 2:00 A.M. working on the draft. The extra effort showed up in complete success the next day.

"Canada is wrong in insisting it is a young country," he declared. "Youth means inexperience and lack of judgment. How can this fit a nation that pushed a railway through the Rockies, developed the prairies and is steadily pushing the last frontier northward?"

2

From the skyscrapers of Toronto and industrial Windsor, Lilibet and Philip went north to inspect a gigantic papermill and flew then to Western Canada.

In Calgary they encountered their first snow and watched the rodeo, wrapped in electrically heated blankets. To the crowd's delight, Philip donned a ten-gallon Stetson hat with which he had been presented, though he noted with private amusement it had been made in London, England.

In the Rockies snow swirls shut out all but a few glimpses of the mountain peaks. In Vancouver, the couple spent twelve and fourteen hours a day on a public schedule and, after a rainy welcome in Victoria, they enjoyed a three-day rest at Eagle Crest Lodge, a log-built country home that might possibly be described as "Balmoral, Canadian-style."

Rain kept them indoors a good deal. One day they decided to go fishing, but a gale blew up, and they had quite a time in the heavy swells that surged through the Straits of Georgia. Philip and Elizabeth characteristically refused to turn back. Happily all went well. And eight young salmon they and their aides landed made a delicious lunch.

After the interlude came the arduous return trip across the prairies, and it became obvious that the homeward program was to be as strenuous as the outward-bound one had been.

Oil refineries in Edmonton; a Sunday church service in Saskatoon, where the Duke delivered the lesson; a Sunday afternoon plane trip to an air training center at Rivers . . . these flashed by. At the air base, incidentally, my cousins met one hundred fifteen hospitalized servicemen who had a special reason for remembering that day for the rest of their lives. Originally, they had been due to meet the Princess at Winnipeg and had been disappointed when her visit to their hospital was limited to a one-minute stop at the door. To make up for it, Philip arranged for them to be driven one hundred fifty-five miles to the Rivers base so that Elizabeth could see and talk to them there.

Reading the reports of the trip in bed in England, Uncle Bertie was rightly pleased at such gestures. And any Canadians who thought the monarchy effete were impressed despite themselves by a particularly full day for Elizabeth and Philip that began at 9:00 A.M. in Port Arthur and ended at 11:30 P.M. in Montreal.

The royal couple drove through Port Arthur (complete with the trimmings of guard-of-honor inspection, bouquet presentation and address of welcome) and toured a grainery.

Then they went on similar tours in Fort William and North Bay before flying to Montreal for a round of presentations and a ninety-minute drive through the city. The following day, a second long drive was made through ranks of cheering Montreal crowds.

An official riding with them wrote to me later that he often had to close his eyes to ward off dizziness; he could not tell how the two of them managed to keep smiling and waving.

This inside point of view reminds me of the wide differences between the newspaper reports of the experiences of the royal couple and what someone, in their position, actually observed and felt. The disparity was nowhere greater than when they finally left Canada and came to the United States.

The biggest demonstration of the North American trip is supposed to have occurred in Washington, where the press estimated that more than a half-million people lined the streets to greet them. But I know that Philip found this a police-ridden and most unresponsive crowd.

Yet, according to the ecstatic newspaper and radio accounts (perhaps prepared the day before), the Princess and Philip, supposedly, could not have imagined they would have such a wonderful welcome. The motorcycle escort, riding ahead with sirens blaring, is said to have drowned the constant chant from thousands of throats of "Philip! Lizzie! Lil! Phil!" In reality, the crowd seemed awed, and there was almost a silence on the way from National Airport to Blair House.

Blair House, on the contrary, was most hospitable. It had become President Truman's residence during repairs to the White House. And here, thanks to circumstance, the pattern of family kinship once again asserted itself. Just as Philip followed Peter as a guest at Balmoral, so Philip and Lilibet now followed my husband as royal state guests at this charming American home.

Peter remembered rising some three hours before breakfast to prepare for his day. Philip got up just as early to anticipate an informal visit to the National Academy of Sciences. Later for the Princess and Philip came the truly appalling reception line at the British Embassy when, in two hours, they shook hands with eighteen hundred people.

This greeting was, of course, an absurd and impossible task. Philip tried to slow it by stopping to talk to every tenth person in line. When the two royal guests might have become giddy, the affair was halted while they had a cup of tea. After two hours the file still curled across the ballroom out of sight but Philip now says, with calm satisfaction, "I seem to remember we finished it!"

It was a relief, I imagine, to return to Canada for a short pause in the Laurentians and a calm journey through the Maritimes.

By then, they had traveled ten thousand miles in Canada, and visited every province of the Dominion. They had spent over five thousand miles in lurching trains and driven eight hundred miles through the overwhelming shock waves of shouting, almost hysterical crowds. It was estimated that they had both shaken official hands at the rate of one or two thousand a week through five weeks and heard the National Anthem two hundred times. The tour demonstrated to Philip broader public acclamation than he ever had thought possible.

They had enjoyed the panorama of a wonderful land of prairies and forests and mountains, spurting oil wells and immense mineral wealth. At the end one could detect the close collaboration of the Princess and the Duke in the words of Elizabeth's farewell broadcast: "I am grateful for the glimpse you have given me of the greatness of this nation and the even greater future which is within its grasp. I have seen this future in the eyes of thousands of your children, and have heard it in their voices."

As they left St. John's in a tender to transfer to their anchored liner, heavy seas and wind piled up into a raging gale. It was a wonderfully dramatic departure. At a dinner party I was told that, although Elizabeth was unaffected, Philip was terribly seasick. But when I ventured to ask him about it, Philip remarked with asperity, "You were told wrong."

3

A new honor awaited Elizabeth and Philip when they returned home. Uncle Bertie approved that Philip should now have his own personal Standard and, at the end of November, he wrote to Elizabeth: "To mark the return to this country from your and Philip's most successful visit to Canada, I propose to have you introduced into the Privy Council, in other words to make you both Privy Counsellors."

The Privy Council has been described as the residual form of the old governing body of Norman England. The Monarch can only act through it and Lilibet and Philip now had to take the traditional oath: that they would advise the King to the best of their discretion, advise for the King's honor without partiality and keep secret his counsel.

New vistas of work and experience were, in any case, opening for them both. Two days after they had left for Canada, it was announced that the King and Queen could not undertake their tour of Australia and New Zealand the following year and that Elizabeth and Philip would go instead.

As a matter of fact, Uncle Bertie's improved health considerably cheered the transatlantic travelers when they returned home. Apart from a troublesome cough, which in time disappeared, the King had come through his illness well; and a sense of relief descended on them all.

Philip flung himself with gusto into the preparations for the new Australian tour, adding fresh towns to the list, and ironing out difficulties in the program that now he could foresee thanks to his Canadian experiences. His spare hours became devoted to the study of Australian affairs and he even paid an impromptu visit to the London Wool Exchange to increase his sheep-farming knowledge and vocabulary.

Between his one great tour satisfactorily concluded and the next one looming, he also went to Durham to inaugurate a new university building and to Stoke-on-Trent to open new laboratories of the pottery trade.

One day he was an honorary Doctor of Laws at London University and another day he sat with the Hebrew elders at a service in the oldest synagogue in Britain. The renewed round of inspections, dinners and sporting events was matched with the happiness of once more being home at Clarence House, enjoying whenever possible the pleasure of playing with the children. Within a few months Philip's term of naval service would qualify him for promotion to commander and it seemed likely that he would go to sea in 1953 with his own destroyer.

We know that the event was not to occur, but the prospect made Christmas particularly bright. Sandringham that year was gay and festive and saw one of the biggest house parties since the war. Peter and I received heartening news that the doctors were very much satisfied with Uncle Bertie's progress. Philip felt that, for both his wife and himself, he could count on intense phases of public service relieved by periods of comparative obscurity and freedom during his naval service.

The original plans for the Commonwealth tour called for departure on the *Gothic*, but Lilibet was anxious to see the royal lodge at Sagana, her wedding gift from the people of Kenya, and to spend a little time there. Therefore, the advance *Gothic* party sailed from Southampton on January 12, 1952, while my cousins remained at Sandringham, Philip going out shooting with Uncle Bertie.

On January 30, for a family farewell party, they all went together to see *South Pacific* at the Drury Lane Theater. At noon the following day, as they exchanged final words before take-off, Uncle Bertie cautioned: "Look out for yourselves." Then Lilibet and Philip left aboard their airliner.

They landed in Nairobi on February 1, and that afternoon attended a garden party. The next day, they visited the National Park, where they were lucky enough to take some pictures of a lion, lioness and cubs gamboling over the rocks. Then, on Sunday, they drove ninety miles upcountry, through Kenya's red dust, to the Sagana Lodge.

The place delighted them. The lodge proved to be nothing more than a six-room bungalow, built of cedar, on stone foundations, and the smell of cooking had drifted hospitably from the kitchen as they pulled in.

Philip and the Princess were out riding at dawn next day to enjoy the magnificent views of forest and mountain; a polo match was arranged for the Duke on the excellent turf at nearby Nyeri. Then, on February 5, they departed for Treetops, the famous observation lodge built in a fig tree in the jungle, to spend the afternoon and the night filming and observing the wild life at a waterhole a few yards distant.

It was a unique experience for them both, far from the maddening crowd. When they left their car they had to walk a half mile to Treetops up the hill through dense cover.

All around, the air was rent by the trumpeting of elephants. As the Princess and Philip reached the observation lodge and the steep access ladder, a herd was clustered only ten yards away. Indeed, the visitors had to walk near the shrilling and belligerent beasts to reach the safety of the ladder and their hosts and guide viewed the larger bulls anxiously.

The sight of the elephant herd was indeed so wonderful that the Princess began filming it as soon as she reached the balcony in the tree.

The future was so unsuspected that Philip and Lilibet planned a running commentary of the jungle film they were making to entertain Uncle Bertie and they reckoned they had the greatest good luck.

They saw a cow elephant suckling her young and afterward giving one of the babies a swimming lesson. They saw an old bull blowing dust out through its trunk to alarm a flock of doves and they watched a battle to the death between two water bucks. They photographed the sporting baboons and a group of wart hogs. Later, as the sunset, they talked to their guide about Uncle Bertie, truly eased by his recovery.

After dinner, watching the waterhole from the balcony, Lilibet and Philip were rewarded by the stealthy movements of a herd of rhino. When the moon set, and the frogs were silent, they retired to their two camp beds, but they were up at daybreak, drinking hot tea and testing the light for more pictures. The guide remarked with amusement that the Princess was the only member of her royal family who had ever slept in a tree.

They did not know that during their carefree hours in a treetop in the jungle, Uncle Bertie had died and in the dark night Elizabeth had become a Queen.

Chapter 11

◆ "Your Liege Man"

1

THE EVENTS of the next few hours can be told only as I heard of them in the family. Philip was taking a siesta in the hot African afternoon when Michael Parker aroused him to tell him that the King was dead. His immediate shocked response was that he could not think it possible.

It turned out that the news had been telephoned to the lodge only on the strength of a news-agency flash from London, and Philip insisted that the report should be confirmed before he told his wife. During the next hour he had to keep the terrible secret to himself while Elizabeth suggested carefree plans for riding out the next morning to see the dawn.

Waiting in suspense, he made an excuse to get her into the

garden out of earshot of the telephone. This ruse succeeded but presently she returned to her room where it fell to Philip alone to tell her her father was dead and she was Queen.

Elizabeth was pale but composed when her private secretary, Martin Charteris, had to ask her by what name she wished to be known as Sovereign.

Her first thought was the need of sending messages of consolation to her mother and her sister. Philip deemed it best to draw her away from the desk and into the open air, and he led her away from the house and took her slowly along the bank of the trout stream that ran through the grounds. As I heard in the family afterward, the Queen did not trust herself to speak for fear of tears.

King Peter and I were in Paris when we ourselves first heard the awful news. After sending our own telegrams we could only sympathetically follow in the newspapers the sad story of our cousin's journey home, the flight in the small African bush-hopping plane to Entebbe and then the night of threatening thunderstorms through which they flew in the B.O.A.C. airliner *Atalanta*. It was not till much later that we heard the fuller details—of the African chauffeur who had impulsively prostrated himself to kiss the feet of his Queen, of the long lines of natives standing silently, heads bowed, along the roads to the first tiny airfield.

Philip for days felt stunned, as if he were anaesthetized. He was consort to the Queen and, in the first hours of shock, could well have echoed Prince Albert's despairing entry in an early diary, "O, the future!" At London Airport, with deliberate formality, he lingered in the plane for a moment or two while the Queen alone slowly went down the steps to her waiting Ministers.

At Clarence House, indeed, he found that State officials already needed to see the Queen on urgent business. At Sandringham he walked behind the coffin as it was carried on an estate wagon to the chapel in the grounds.

Meanwhile a formal black-edged letter arrived, bidding us to the funeral. The day before the procession to Windsor, Peter and I made our own last homage. We went into Westminster Hall by a side door. Instead of flying at a masthead, the Royal Standard was draped now over a coffin. The Imperial State Crown and the pieces of the Regalia twinkled with terrible impersonality in the artificial candlelight.

At St. George's Chapel, Windsor, standing close to Uncle Palo and other members of the Royal Family, I found it still hard to realize that the sad wailing of the bagpipes was for Uncle Bertie.

The next morning I had to return to Paris and meet Alexander, who was flying from America. Peter remained in London and soon went to lunch at Clarence House. He was alarmed to find how thin Elizabeth had grown since their last meeting, and that Philip seemed withdrawn. The two men maintained the conversation by talking about me, but Peter wanted so much to find words of sympathy for the young new Queen and finally he found an opportunity. He said, simply, "I know what it's like!"

She gave a wan little smile and replied gently. "Yes, Peter, I know you do. Thank you. It helps."

Philip accompanied Peter to the car, a moment when there might have been confidences man to man, but the conversation remained deliberately casual. "You could feel it all underneath," said Peter to me later. "It was as if a volcano had been covered." He paused and added, thoughtfully, "I don't know how long he can last . . . bottled up like that!"

2

Naturally a good deal of discussion went on among Philip's relatives at this time about his future. My Aunt Helen, Marina's mother, who was a great stickler for points of precedence and etiquette, pointed out that, when his wife was not present, Philip came below the Dukes of Gloucester and Windsor. Presumably this was his status as a junior royal duke yet, strictly speaking, the ruling house now bore his name: it was the House of Mountbatten and both the heir to the throne, Prince Charles, and his sister, Princess Anne, were Mountbattens.

These technicalities were not revised until the Declaration in Council when the Queen resumed for herself and her descendants the name of Windsor.

Philip's naval status, however, also gave rise to anachronisms. His promotion to commander, for which he was qualified in terms of service time, did not come until July 1952. He had always dearly wanted to earn his promotion and Elizabeth waited until then before heaping on him the ranks of Admiral of the Fleet, Field Marshal and Marshal of the Royal Air Force, though they had to come.

The precedents and injunctions of the Prince Consort, of course, filled many conversations, with Aunt Helen reminding us that Albert had not actually been given that title for seventeen years.

None of us could imagine Philip submerging his forceful personality in full deference to Elizabeth nor following Albert's self-effacing dictum, "The position of Prince Consort requires that the husband should entirely sink his own individual existence in that of his wife; that he should . . . shun all attention . . . assume no separate responsibility before the public, but make his position entirely a part of hers."

As a matter of fact, Albert went a little further in a letter to the Duke of Wellington in which he declared, "As natural head of her family, superintendant of her household, manager of her private affairs, sole confidential adviser in politics and only assistant in her communications with the officers of her government, he is besides the husband of the Queen, the tutor of the royal children, the private secretary of the Sovereign and her permanent Minister."

Philip, having read two or three biographies of the Prince Consort, was neither deterred nor influenced by his ghostly predecessor. Albert had refused a peerage because it was beneath his dignity, but one couldn't help but remember that Philip had refused a "Royal Highness" from Uncle Bertie in order to become plain Lieutenant Mountbatten.

Only a week or two after Uncle Bertie's funeral, Philip symbolized his future course when he slipped away from Clarence House one evening—the place was in a turmoil of packing—and spent four hours in the House of Commons listening to a debate. He made his interests more apparent when he visited the House again to hear the Chancellor of the Exchequer's budget speech.

That March Philip became the first member of the Royal Family to fly in a jet plane. He went up in a Comet, when it was still undergoing flight tests (well before anyone knew of the structural deficiencies that were to plague this ship).

When Philip toured the Lancashire coalfields and agreed to inspect a mine, he was engaging in a venerable royal tradition, yet he embued the visit with new touches. I read that he had been frisked for cigarettes and matches, the usual newspaper description. But the full story I learned privately was that he descended two thousand feet into the mine, lurching part of the way in an open bucket, and crawled through one of the furthermost galleries to the coal face. He shared the miners' everyday lunch at their canteen, and they banged their mugs for him in approval. It was no coincidence that, the next day, the pit had a record output.

The discipline of visits to mines, workshops, research laboratories and the like, enlivened by his unwillingness to make them routine, was Philip's support during these tense early months of his new life. He wanted to demonstrate that he knew what was going on. But sometimes he pushed himself too far.

Shortly after moving to Buckingham Palace, he came in to breakfast one morning looking so yellow that Elizabeth insisted on calling the Palace's resident doctor. Philip had jaundice. He would have to spend three weeks in bed, at which he was, naturally, much disgusted. He was confined in a temporary sickroom where he was watched by a set of depressing pictures of Spanish grandees looking almost as yellow as he was.

Fortunately, those three weeks, followed by a short holiday at Balmoral, soon set him up again and were just what he needed. He returned to harness eager, brisk and confident. If involvement is, as they say, a prime ingredient of happiness, Philip was henceforward and ever after a happy man.

The foremost among his new responsibilities was undoubtedly his appointment as chairman of the Coronation Commission. Even my Aunt Mary was at a loss to find any precedent for a Queen Regnant appointing her husband in effect to be general manager of her crowning.

It is known, of course, that the Duke of Norfolk as hereditary Earl Marshal was the master strategist of the Coronation ceremony, but the Commission was the working committee, and among many responsibilities it was concerned with Commonwealth relations.

Philip was also made a member of the Court of Claims, the ancient tribunal that examined those claiming an historic right to perform special services for the Queen on her Coronation, and he was elected president of the committee to advise the Royal Mint on the design of the new seals, coins and medals.

Just as a motion picture has a producer and a director, so Philip was trebly a power behind the Coronation scenes. Moreover, just as the Coronation was a masterly enactment of ancient tradition, so Philip saw to it that there were innovations to give it the clear stamp of our own time.

Early one morning his thoroughness led him onto the famous balcony of Buckingham Palace where he pretended to study the sky with the weight of an imaginary crown on his head.

When the experts gathered to decide the precise route and height of the ceremonial fly past, he was prepared to show them that it would be impossible for the Queen to raise her head to look at the sky immediately above her and still keep her crown securely in place.

From stage to stage, Philip insisted on the maximum Commonwealth symbolism in the forthcoming ceremony.

One suggestion was that the hundred new-minted shillings with which the Queen redeems the Sword of State should come from all nations of the Commonwealth. This had to be ruled out because the coinage could not be manufactured in time.

But Philip discovered, on scrutinizing the items of the Regalia, that two golden bracelets which had been part of the crowning jewelry for many years had never been worn by a Sovereign in modern times.

Ultimately, two new bracelets were accepted as the gift of the Commonwealth governments and were introduced into the ceremony as a symbol of the Queen's bond with her peoples.

Far from following tradition to the letter, the Coronation was enhanced, in fact, by many felicitous departures. I would not like to give the impression that Philip in any sense ran the show, for the task was beyond the scope of any single person. Yet he was indeed head of all the Coronation plans, and not content to make this a nominal role. After reading widely in Coronation history, he covered thoroughly every detail of the arrangements, literally from precautions against forged invitations to the interior illumination of the ancient, golden coach.

The part he would play in the actual procession remained undefined for a time. It was debated whether he should have a separate coach or ride with the Queen. His processional place had no precedent since the crowning of Queen Anne, who had been carried to the Abbey in a chair and whose consort had walked—some say tottered—just ahead of the nobles holding the Regalia.

Philip coped with another specific problem, that of the ingredients of the oil with which Elizabeth was to be anointed. Part of the oil blended for Queen Victoria had been preserved for more than a century, serving in several coronations, but the last precious drops had ebbed away when the deanery of Westminster Abbey was bombed in 1941.

The former royal chemists, he thought, should have the prescription on their books, but it developed that they had gone out of business.

The original recipe used for Charles II gave some forty ingredients, including myrrh, orange flowers, cinnamon, musk and sweet calamus, but still omitted to name the all-important, basic compounding oil. The mystery was finally cleared up when someone remembered that a former director of the chemists' firm had boasted of a souvenir he had at home.

From a country house in Kent Philip retrieved a vial of four ounces of the oil used for Victoria. Two ounces were consecrated and set aside for Queen Elizabeth. The rest he had preserved for the sacred rites of the distant future.

From his point of view, one of the little things that went wrong was also one of the things that went right. Early in 1953, thousands of pictures, mugs and other Coronation souvenirs, showing him in the uniform of a Commander, had been manufactured and distributed throughout the world at a time when he already had been made Admiral of the Fleet. But my cousin took secret pleasure, I believe, in having publicized irrevocably the highest naval rank he had himself earned.

In reality, one of Philip's first honors of the new reign caused some little amusement among his relatives. This was when he heard that Elizabeth had appointed him Ranger of Windsor Great Park. What did it mean? Was it a joke? We did not know. I remember some fun we had at his expense suggesting a suitable costume he might wear for the post.

Elizabeth and Philip had derived some very real fun themselves from seeing the new royal cipher of the Crown and the letters E.R. on the Windsor milk bottles.

But it went against the grain with Philip to receive honors or titles for which he had no qualification. He was not too happy about being a Field Marshal.

Sir Winston Churchill told us on one occasion of the situation surrounding Philip's wish to learn to fly. Without a pilot's license, Philip had pointed out, he would have to undergo the absurdity of wearing his formal R.A.F. uniform without wings. He went on to argue his case for saving time on one-day engagements as well as the advantages of being able to take the controls in emergency. Both my husband and Prince Bernhard of the Netherlands were cited in this regard. Sir Winston did not oppose the Prince too strenuously. This was another of those jobs that had to be mastered, and indeed Philip was impatient with delay.

Air advisers thought that it might be best to wait till the spring of Coronation year. Philip pointed out that there were many days of fair weather in the winter and offered to be available for training whenever possible. When the weather prospects were good, I'm told, he got up an hour earlier in order to fit the lessons into his schedule.

He began his training early in November 1952, and did his first solo flight just before Christmas that year. This seems to me pretty good going, though Peter tells me it is standard timing. Two months later, Philip made his first loop, and then transferred to heavier, faster planes. His final handling test was in April and the following month the graduate flew over Windsor in an extracurricular flight. He thus received his wings a month before the Coronation and just a few weeks before his thirty-second birthday. Precisely a week before the Coronation he flew himself by helicopter from the lawns of Buckingham Palace to a review of Commonwealth troops, which was almost a symbolic act of his own achievement.

Meanwhile, by a warrant issued in September 1952, the Queen had already ordained that "His Royal Highness, Philip, Duke of Edinburgh" should "henceforth upon all occasions and in all Meetings except where otherwise provided by Act of Parliament have, hold and enjoy Place, Pre-eminence and Precedence next to Her Majesty."

This publicly regulated Philip's precedence, although the confidential booklet of the Royal Household, "Precedence at Court," had already defined it some months beforehand.

At the same time, the Civil List provision for Philip had been discussed by a House of Commons committee at great length and fixed at an annuity of £40,000 ($110,000), subject to tax. Once again this seemed rather niggardly to me, for it was only £10,000 more than the sum accorded tax-free to Albert, Prince Consort, in spite of the immense changes that the passing of a century had wrought in purchasing power.

Curiously enough, the entire Civil List for the Queen was only £5,000 a year more than the provision for her great-grandfather, King Edward VII. So far as I know, Philip has never commented to anyone about his financial provision, although he soon required a great deal of iron determination and ingenuity to keep within the budget.

The crowded events of the sixteen months between the Accession and the Coronation really left little time for taking stock. These ranged, for Philip, from a short flight to Malta to present colors to the Royal Marines Commando Brigade to a visit to Cambridge to receive that University's honorary degree of Doctor of Laws.

It was over ten years, I could not help reflecting when he got his LL.D., since my husband had been forced to relinquish his own law studies at Cambridge to grapple alone with the political problems of his mangled, divided country.

But there were deeper echoes for Philip in turn, I felt, when he took part in Elizabeth's first State Opening of Parliament, in the role of a husband supporting his wife. Now the Queen sat on her isolated golden throne while Philip retired to the gold-studded Chair of State in which Prince Albert had once sat. I do not know how Victoria and Albert occupied themselves after their State Openings, but it is a matter of history that Elizabeth and Philip returned to the Palace, changed their clothes and went to a children's party.

"So what?" said Philip, when I tried to compliment him with a "Good for you!" But it seemed to me a symbol of the simple, democratic lives they intended to maintain.

3

Taking stock of 1953, I will always remember my thirty-second birthday, for, with my greeting cards, there came a newspaper with the headlines that Aunt May (Queen Mary) had died. Once again Philip was following an honored gun carriage, and yet one could not help having a curious feeling in the midst of the mourning that this death had a propriety.

It was as if the new reign, the Elizabethan era, were starting with a slate of its own, freed from its ties with the old.

Just two weeks later, the new royal yacht was launched and named *Britannia*. Thus event followed event. And, as all the world turned its eyes toward London, Elizabeth and Philip, the bustle of Coronation preparations settled into final rehearsals.

Innumerable lesser royalties jostled to be guests, but this was one ceremony of family importance that Peter and I could not be privileged to see, for Queen Victoria had established the precedent that no foreign crowned head should attend the Coronation of a British monarch.

On the other hand, fate offered us an appropriate alternative. We were in Paris, and when, for the first time, the exclusive male sanctum of the Travellers Club opened its door to women, I was invited to come with Peter to watch the great occasion on television.

I was truly deeply moved as we saw our two cousins, Elizabeth and Philip, conducted through the ritual.

What else could I feel, as a Queen, but the utmost reverence and a deep-flowing sympathy as I watched the Archbishop slowly and solemnly place the crown on Elizabeth's head? I heard the great cry of "God Save the Queen!" and in the triumphant trumpets there was for me an undertone recollecting the shout, "God Save the King," that I had heard for my husband at gatherings of loyal Yugoslavs.

My eyes could not turn from the screen as Philip came forward in his own magnificent robes and knelt in homage to swear the ancient oath, "to become your liege man of life and limb, and of earthly worship; and faith and truth I will bear unto you, to live and die, against all manner of folks. So help me God."

Rising, he mounted the steps of the throne, touched the crown with his hand and kissed Elizabeth's left cheek. As he did so, he disturbed the crown just a little, so that Elizabeth had to adjust it on her head.

It was at that moment that I thought of Uncle Andrea. He had lived in the Travellers Club and now we were sitting in the very room where he had so often sat and we were watching his son, invested with every splendor, moving through perhaps the greatest ritual of sacrament to be enacted anywhere in the world in the twentieth century.

Chapter 12

◆ World Tour for Two

1

FOR MOST of us the Coronation ended when the last decorations were taken down or as the freshness faded from the family topic of conversation, but for Elizabeth and Philip the ripples of recognition and acclaim spread in widening circles, from the investitures and banquets at the Palace to the State drives through London, and from the exacting ceremonial of Trooping the Color to the Royal Review of the Fleet.

Again and again, late on Coronation Day, my cousins had appeared on the Palace balcony to acknowledge the ever-cheering crowd.

From London the wonderful waves of enthusiasm buoyed

them both through the Coronation visit to Scotland and the further visits to Northern Ireland and Wales.

On a day in late June, Prince Philip attended an investiture at the Palace in the morning, went on to the Test Cricket Match at Lord's before lunch, was at London Airport in the early afternoon to see Aunt Elizabeth and Princess Margaret off on their tour of Rhodesia, and later put in an appearance at Wimbledon to watch the tennis.

I was remote from these activities, but I saw clearly that Prince Philip had fully and satisfactorily adapted himself to the intensive new pressures of his environment and position.

Probably the only cloud on the horizon lay in the appalling publicity that was given at this time to the friendship of Group Captain Peter Townsend and Princess Margaret.

Philip disliked this midsummer speculation intensely, just as he disliked anything that could diminish the dignity of the Crown.

On the other hand, the official attitude he took toward the relationship must have clashed with the tolerant philosophy he once held that everybody must lead the life he or she thinks best. But at this time I also had troubles of my own and I must make it clear that this was an interlude when I was not in my cousin's confidence.

I do know that it was as dismaying to him that these difficulties should have occured in Coronation year as it was a delight that his mother, Aunt Alice, attended the ceremony, fervently sharing its religious emotion and enjoying its unexcelled pageantry.

Except for a break at Balmoral there was no reprieve in the incessant stream of engagements all that summer. Although Philip managed to get in some sailing at Cowes, it was to the usual accompaniment of boatloads of photographers. (By con-

trast, he reported, the unprofessional people were most considerate.)

Still wider developments were soon shaping in the royal tour
of Australia and New Zealand, which had been planned and
canceled three times. The journey had been scheduled twice
for King George VI and Aunt Elizabeth, and twice postponed
on account of Uncle Bertie's illness. Elizabeth and Philip had
set out instead, only to be recalled from Kenya the first week
because of the King's death.

This time the projected itinerary was extended to a vast overseas tour longer than any royal progress of modern times. When
Philip boarded the B.O.A.C. airliner *Canopus* the night of November 23, 1953, he knew that all being well, Elizabeth and he
would travel over forty thousand miles, visit twelve different territories of the Commonwealth, observing and being seen, receive
the plaudits of untold millions and, hopefully, give them great
pleasure in return.

The major change in schedule, I noted, was that Philip had
reversed the order of the tour from back to front.

For a time, after the Accession, we had taken it for granted
that the Queen would one day resume the journey via Kenya as
it originally had started, but Philip, like a good husband, saw at
once that such a trip would evoke too many painful memories.
Also the hazards of the Mau Mau campaign of terror were considered too great, and the program was altered completely.

So instead of flying eastward across Africa, the *Canopus* carried Elizabeth westward over the Atlantic. It was the first time
a reigning queen had flown the Atlantic, and, strung out far
beneath the plane, eight ships kept constant vigil.

In the middle of the night, Philip woke up, puzzled to hear
distant shouts of "We Want the Queen!" and "Come out,
Phil!" For a moment he thought he was dreaming. The plane

had touched down at Gander at 3:25 A.M. and even there, at that unearthly hour, people were waiting.

Philip and the Queen got up and dressed to acknowledge this unofficial reception and then wisely returned to snatch what sleep they could. But then Philip got up early again, going forward to the cockpit and gazing down on the panorama of islands glittering in the dawn.

2

At this point, as I scan the notes I have jotted down about Philip's world travels, I confess I find myself in a quandary. There are details passed on from relatives and friends who insist on anonymity, as if it were quite shocking to assist in the private chronicling of history.

There are jottings I have made myself in my journals, though they are often no more than a word or two as an *aide-mémoire*.

It would be absurd to pretend that I have always followed my cousin's innumerable tours and travels with unwavering attention. I cannot hope to record them day by day, week by week, or even a thousand miles at a time. The round-the-world tour of 1953 and 1954, for instance, saw four thousand miles traversed by car and jeep in seven hundred different drives and excursions. Eighteen thousand miles were covered by aircraft and even more than this distance by sea.

At Gander, as I have said, the travelers dressed in the middle of the night over their night clothes to respond to greetings while, in Bermuda, they were kept awake by the croaking of bullfrogs. They rose before dawn to face a busy day and the next night were lulled to sleep in Jamaica by the songs of the people.

But Philip was everywhere resilient and quick to share a joke, and he quickly brought to the tour his own special geniality and drive.

At first a great deal went wrong and, reliant as he was on his hosts, there was not much Philip could do. At Government House, Bermuda, thirty of the island's leading citizens attended a welcome dinner which caused great criticism because, in a population nearly two-thirds colored, there was not a colored person among the guests. The *cause célèbre* seemed hardly justified for half those present at a garden party that afternoon were colored.

In Jamaica, an over-exuberant schoolmaster attempted a Sir Walter Raleigh act by throwing his coat before the Queen though there wasn't a puddle in sight. The man was hustled away by the police, and I can imagine Philip's unhappiness, later aboard the *Gothic*, when he heard that the man had been charged under the Lunacy Laws.

Then, in Panama, Philip experienced the most fantastic and probably one of the most frightening welcomes of his life. The police had concentrated their forces on center points but completely neglected to line the royal route. As soon as the dancing, yelling crowds realized there was nothing to stop them, they surged off the pavements into the road.

The Duke and the Queen had been placed in separate cars, and Philip was very much alarmed to see his wife's automobile, as well as his own open car, slowed to a walking pace by the frenzied human sea. Running alongside, ringing handbells, even trying to jump on the cars, the spectators went wild with enthusiasm. Soon passenger cars began cutting in from side streets and the procession was halted completely.

Equerries and police finally organized a sort of football interference to help Philip leave his stranded vehicle and join the

Queen in a closed car. This move proved providential for another reason altogether. Shortly afterward, a torrential rainstorm lashed down. It did not dampen the high spirits of the crowd or scatter them, but the Queen and Philip slowly drove on, protected, through the sodden marsh of humanity.

3

Three weeks after leaving London the travelers arrived in the Fiji Islands, and the writer of a diary that has been lent to me wrote the memo, "Duke on hot seat." At a sports field Philip sat down in a leather armchair that had been baking in the sun for hours and leaped up again with unroyal speed. Seated on a canvas chair brought from the shade, it was Elizabeth's turn to jump when two files of hefty Fijians lined up in front of her armed with three-foot clubs and then hurled themselves at each other in a mad war dance.

To heighten the effect, a ceremonial draught of kava—the native drink—had first been brewed before the visitors' eyes.

"You will find it tastes like soap!" Philip warned the Queen as she was handed the potion in half a coconut shell.

The Queen drained it bravely.

After Fiji came Tonga where the beaming welcome from Queen Salote, and the exotic feast spread on the ground before the visitors, would long live in their memory. The banquet had no leftovers, for when the official guests retired, the tables were thrown open to the general public and in a short time not a yam nor a joint of roast pork remained.

Philip reported home, with amusement, that the local musicians had played the flute by blowing their noses and that when a return dinner was staged for Queen Salote at the little British Consulate, the lights failed. I gathered his fingers were itching to help fix them. But it was not until New Zealand that he had his first opportunity to show how he could personally enhance the success of the tour.

Unexpected tragedy greeted the royal arrival in Auckland. On Christmas Eve, a railway bridge had collapsed into a flooded river, carrying with it a crowded train in which one hundred sixty-six people were killed. It was the worst rail disaster that New Zealand had ever known, and there was scarcely a family in the country who did not know someone involved in the awful accident.

The Prime Minister spoke for the Dominion when he asked the Queen not to change her program and, apart from a visit to a family of survivors to hear their story from their own lips, the tour superficially went on as usual.

Yet one morning Philip rose at 5:00 A.M., after a previous night's dinner that had lasted till midnight, to fly three hundred miles to attend the mass funeral service in Wellington. The journey had been the Prime Minister's suggestion but Philip had readily agreed. Considerations of fatigue were set aside, as they always must be, though one can sympathetically record that he snatched a cat nap as he flew back after the service to rejoin the Queen. They had engagements that evening and he in fact ended up with thirty-six hours of official duties on only five hours of real sleep.

A day or two earlier, the Duke had heard of differences between the Government and the Waikato tribe of Maoris, who were affronted that the Queen was not scheduled to enter their meeting house. In fact the itinerary had allowed too little time. But Philip solved the problem in his own way. The royal cars stopped. The address of welcome was chanted. But just before they turned back to the car he nodded at the meeting house and murmured, "Couldn't we just take a peep?"

Loud Maori cheers greeted this genial move. It was nothing, and it was everything. The tour would have been an immense solo triumph for Elizabeth but Philip's watchfulness underlined the success most decisively.

On occasions grave and gay he constantly lightened the ceremonies with a friendly gesture or a humorous aside. In one town the people placed behind a dais could not see him and a man shouted, "Where's the Duke?" Characteristically, Philip walked through the official group to smile and wave.

Watching a demonstration of sheep shearing, he was invited to try his hand. "No, thanks," he said, "I might nick it and we've had enough mutton!" Headlines repeated that homely joke and it delighted millions.

It was noted everywhere that Philip always showed a knack of drawing the Queen's attention to the little things in which so much love and loyalty were expressed, details that might have been missed—the tiny station saying it with flowers, the parade of pet lambs, the children waiting on a bridge to dive for pennies to amuse the Queen.

The Maoris gravely appointed Philip their "God of War." At one town he visited a plant research institute and spent two hours discussing pest control, a gesture that made him extremely popular with New Zealand farmers.

In Canterbury province a small boy had written to him with an invitation to see his toy railway. A secretary had replied that it would be a little difficult to alter the tour arrangements but, undeterred, the boy appeared at a wayside station waving his miniature engine and amid the large crowd Philip spotted him.

All these incidents accumulated, as the tour progressed south, into a new and highly individual "projection" of Philip.

At Wellington he read the lessons in the old wooden church of St. Paul's as if he were at home in England, and all New Zealand felt that no more friendly or moving touch could have been contrived. At every point on the tour his practice of helping people spread incalculable good will.

A press correspondent with the tour summed it up: "On how many countless platforms, at how many receptions and balls, on the stage of how many town halls, did he not stop and question and laugh and joke and ease the nervous tension of those who longed, yet dreaded, to meet the majesty of the Queen."

4

In Australia, in Sydney, where the one-time naval lieutenant and his wife were met by ten miles of cheers, in township after township as they swung through New South Wales, the reception was—if possible—even heartier than in New Zealand.

I used to read of the tumult through which they passed, and was amazed at their sheer endurance. To be cheered in the streets can be inspiring, I know, but Australia's acclaim was often so fervent that it could be heard miles away. To fit in the maximum number of engagements, Elizabeth and Philip often parted company. The Queen lunched with a women's assembly, while the Duke inspected a university. The Queen went to the races while Philip paid a surprise visit to the Sydney cricket ground. And one night Philip slipped away from it all to visit his old friend, Joe Fallon, who, not dreaming he would come, was in pajamas on the point of going to bed.

Officials worried needlessly, I think, when students at Melbourne University staged a "rag" or party for Philip. He remained the master of the occasion. Presented pluckily with a pair of crutches, he handed them right back, commenting, "Your need is greater than mine."

Philip helped the Queen open the Federal Parliament in Canberra. But he also wanted to show her the Australia of his midshipman days. One afternoon he drove her to a sheep station, asking specially for a car with private number plate, just for old times' sake.

In Tasmania, also, he arranged to stay with the Queen at a private home near Launceston, where he had enjoyed hospitality on a wartime leave. Philip's desire to share his past with Elizabeth was never more evident. He wished her to know the soft green foothills and the friendly faces, and to remember them as he did.

Then the tour swung through Melbourne, Ballarat, Brisbane, Toowoomba and other cities to Cairns. Here the royal couple reached the furthest point north in Australia and took in the beauties of the Great Barrier Reef; and they made a special visit to one of the tiny coral-edged islets for a day of sunbathing and swimming.

They flew to Adelaide and journeyed through the industrial townships and wine districts. Everywhere the pattern of gaily decorated streets repeated itself—bands playing almost unheard for the roar of cheering, the assembled tributes of a great people.

Perhaps Philip had one of his personally memorable days when he flew to the semi-desert region of Woomera to inspect a missile range and fire off a rocket himself. I can remember that not many years before he and I had watched and marveled at a fireworks display, following a royal celebration in Athens. Now he confronted the power of intercontinental missiles—so enormous are the changes in a twentieth-century lifetime.

The Australian leg of the tour was completed at Perth and

Fremantle. The "Royal Progress," as the papers never ceased to call it, had been the most lavish carnival that had ever interrupted that continent's work and play.

Excitement was at such a pitch that one family camped for a week on a strategic street corner to catch a few seconds' glimpse of the visitors. A zealous politician, for his part, collected royal handshakes until, at the eighth meeting, Philip found him in a hospital presentation line and politely inquired, "In for treatment?"

But the boisterous affection of the crowds was unmistakable. In retrospect, Philip said that it was just as well he and his wife had been prepared for the excitement of the tour by the welcome in Canada and drilled for the parades and the ceremonies by the Coronation season. He felt that the good accomplished by the trip far outweighed the physical exhaustion.

When they finally left Australia on the *Gothic*, they had undergone seven weeks of dizzying experiences. Most of the tour, they found out subsequently, could only be recalled from the movies that Elizabeth had taken.

5

In the family we now took for granted Elizabeth's and Philip's stamina and ability to recuperate swiftly.

Aboard the *Gothic*, Pamela Mountbatten thought they would disappear into their suite to rest for three or four days, but nothing of the kind. Philip showed up at lunch the next day as usual, inquiring, "Hockey at five?"

The game of deck hockey, seven to a side, was his favorite form of shipboard diversion; in it he was invariably energetic, swiping madly at the rope grommet which was used instead of a ball. But he was apparently invulnerable to the flailing sticks and blows that resulted in casualties among the household and reduced most of his playmates to "hockey hobblers."

The days had crossed into April when Elizabeth and Philip next went ashore to visit Home Island in the Cocos-Keeling group. And the welcome there was in sharp contrast to Australia's.

Instead of vast crowds, there were only a few airline personnel and their wives. Instead of inspecting factories and universities, my cousins were shown through a copra shed. But it was a prelude to the splendor of Ceylon, to the change from white faces to brown, from red, white and blue bunting to the pinks and pale greens of the East, from cheers to respectful silence and salaams. It was almost a relief not to have to smile, to be able to sit gravely during royal drives, to walk in dignity to open Parliament accompanied by the music of conch shells and the roll of drums. The visit would have been enchanting but for the overpowering heat.

They were glad to drive into the hills where, oddly enough, Philip found basketfuls of petitions had followed him. His first reaction was to go through all of them, but he soon learned that the average petition sought to redress a wrong done to a great-grandfather in a situation equally ancient. He settled the problem by referring most of them to the Governor-General's staff— where they were in fact given the utmost care.

In contrast to these legal duties came the thrill of the whirling, jingling dancers that greeted the royal arrival in Kandy, capped by a procession the following night when, with one hundred and forty caparisoned elephants, they moved in a torchlit parade watched by a million people.

To anyone but Elizabeth and Philip, I suppose, it would have been an anticlimax to visit the colony of Aden. Here, however,

Philip was fascinated by the new oil refineries and mentioned them afterward as one of the sights of the trip.

Next they flew to Entebbe, the airfield from which Lilibet had begun her flight home as Queen over two years before. In Kenya she had the historic task of opening the sluices of the new Owens Falls Dam to bring power to the heart of central Africa.

The dam can be reckoned a moment of history, but what mattered far more to Elizabeth and Philip, as individuals, was the meeting with their children on the yacht *Britannia* at Tobruk. How Charles and Anne had grown! How wonderful to be with them! These were rapturous minutes, and Elizabeth and Philip bubbled with laughter. They were on board over an hour before they realized they had not even thought of the *Britannia*, in which they were sailing for the first time.

Uncle Bertie had encouraged Philip to join in planning the yacht. Details like the saluting platform and the helicopter deck were Philip's ideas. Now that he was in his stateroom, he found the floodlit model of the frigate *Magpie* mounted on one wall, just as he had ordered. The *Britannia* was, indeed, not the least of their coming-home pleasures, as the royal couple voyaged via Malta and Gibraltar on the last week of their one hundred seventy-three days around the world.

Chapter 13

⟡ A Man's Man

1

PHILIP RETURNED to London with enhanced status anchored by a new law. In his absence, legislation had been passed to make him Regent, should the Queen die while their son, Prince Charles, was still under eighteen. It covered a contingency which no one considered likely. Yet by the Act, Parliament secured Philip's permanent place in the Constitution, and honored him for his many services.

After this acclaim and the rigors of the trip, it might have been excusable if he had taken things easy, but of course he did nothing of the kind.

When I learned of Philip's plans for the rest of the summer, I agreed with a friend who observed he was simply a glutton for punishment. In three months, he was due to visit France, Germany and Canada. While his secretary was typing the final itineraries of these solo trips, he was busy drafting plans for a visit to Nigeria with the Queen to take place the following year.

Nigeria, in turn, shared his desk with immediate arrangements for an industrial study conference at Oxford, schedules for a visit on the *Britannia* to Dartmouth, the program for a State visit to London of the Swedish King and Queen, and timetables for functions as separate as a sherry party for the fiftieth anniversary of the Entente Cordiale and a ceremony aboard the H.M.S. *Wellington* to initiate him as Master of the Honorable Company of Master Mariners.

In addition, he prepared for his public engagements with the Queen: a review of United Kingdom Police Forces at Hyde Park, Garter ceremonies at Windsor, the Trooping of the Color, and the social appearances at Epsom and Ascot.

One evening, the Lord Lieutenants of Britain's ninety counties entertained the Queen and Philip at a dinner at Lancaster House, an event last staged on behalf of a monarch in the nineteenth century. The Lieutenants had debated for months on a suitable gift to present. It had to be something unusual, and I think just the right note was struck when Elizabeth was given a painting of Philip's Act of Homage during the Coronation.

Philip was also absorbed by an important private interest, apart from polo at Cowdray and sailing the *Bluebottle* at Cowes, which was a subject in his animated conversation. It was his concern for royal estate management.

Technically, there are officials and hard-working staffs who operate Sandringham and Balmoral as personal employees of the Queen, and Windsor and Buckingham Palace under the Ministry of Public Works. At first, I rather think Philip had to be careful not to tread on anyone's toes. But by now he was as diplomatic as he was disciplined.

Coming back from the Commonwealth tour, he was eager to discover how some of his innovations had developed. At Buckingham Palace, Philip had made "explorations" through almost all the six hundred rooms. He had asked polite permission to visit the staff rooms. He had found, upon inquiring the duties of practically everyone he met, that arrangements were deplorably old-fashioned. For example, he discovered that ordering a sandwich took the services of four men!

So he had called in a friend from the Savoy Hotel, Hugh Wontner, to reorganize the whole system. An intercom was installed. The kitchen for the family was relocated directly beneath their apartments to give the efficiency of a small private house. When, on getting back home, Philip cajoled a naval friend to inspect this new region, the friend reported that the pressure cookers, time control switches, deep freeze, automatic grills and other equipment made the royal kitchen resemble the galley of a modern luxury yacht.

On the other hand, Philip knew he had to budget his improvements. He is sometimes reported to have an office complete with flashing lights and streamlined decor. But the truth was that, on this occasion, he simply continued his occupancy of the late King's study and left it very much as it was.

Philip had introduced himself into the Sandringham operation too. After being named master of the estate, he toured the farms, sometimes with the manager but more often alone. And by now he had become an expert in the art of framing cheerful but pertinent inquiries.

He trekked out to the saltings where cattle grazed on land reclaimed from the sea, to the nurseries on the slope of Sandringham Hill where young trees are methodically planted, and to the flax mills and vegetable gardens.

It was said later that he was trying to run Sandringham like a battleship. This was nonsense. He passionately wanted familiarity with all details of management, to discover how the estate could be improved. The gardeners who thought that the produce gardens were too extensive and the agent who wanted one of the farms redeveloped found him an unexpected ally. For soon he made plans with them that were put into action.

When the Government closed its flax factory at Sandringham, Philip had the sheds converted into sties for two thousand pigs. Here was bacon produced for profit. And he had come a long way from the days he had let the pigs out of their houses at Panka.

Though four successive kings had used the estate mostly for pleasure, Philip argued and acted successfully to see that the seventeen thousand acres paid for themselves and that they served to offset deficits in other royal properties.

Once, the mudscraper at the Sandringham garden door caught his attention; he noticed that the mud, when scraped off, was carried right back to his boots by the porcupine-like brush. Philip thought about it for a while. Today the "Edinburgh Pole Boot Wiper and Scraper" is being sold at an ex-servicemen's workshop in London—and Philip was the designer.

At Windsor, a number of agricultural journalists were invited to tour the farms to see the improvements themselves. Some of the Prince Consort's bullock yards, they found, had been converted into an area for one thousand chickens stimulated by electric light to rise early and give a long laying day. They saw the Ayrshire herd machine-milked into an assembly line of churns, and the young calves dehorned electrically. Had they come at another time of year they would have seen for themselves that, as Prince Albert had introduced Christmas trees to Britain, Philip was marketing them from Windsor.

2

Philip had been back in Britain only five weeks when he flew to France to call on President Coty, visit Supreme Headquarters of the Allied Forces in Europe and by invitation meet Lord Ismay, the Secretary-General of N.A.T.O.

This two-day visit showed that, although he was severed from politics at home, he felt the responsibility of leadership in international policies that might help the peace.

From Paris he piloted his own plane to Luneburg, Germany, to review the Cameron Highlanders. He left Paris wearing somber battledress and stepped out on the German airfield in the full colors of the Cameron kilt. He later traveled on to Schloss Salem to see his sisters, Sophie and Theodora, and turned up in spruce Sandringham clothes such as Uncle Bertie used to wear.

Sometimes, hearing of Philip's more distant travels, I would remember the small boy who would silently wander off and not be seen for the rest of the afternoon. Several of his recent journeys, it seems to me, have originated in perhaps some grown-up counterpart to that mood of boyhood solitude.

As early as 1952 he agreed to open the Empire Games in Vancouver, and the plans developed into an air visit to the massive new industrial developments of the Canadian North. By July 28, 1954, when he flew outward-bound from Tangmere, in an R.C.A.F. plane, the schedule had become another highly concentrated tour (ten thousand miles in twenty days) and a demonstration of his interest, as it was said, in the projects of Canadian muscle and American capital. I felt that the prospects of solitude had been swamped in the planning but the inner-most mood had assumed a new significance.

Though it was a fact-finding royal tour with the aim of view-ing the Canadian people at work, it was also a lone-wolf tour, the first of the many great journeys that Philip, ever more mobile than the Queen, was to undertake by himself to all parts of the world.

He was truly inspired by the thought of doing a meaningful job for the monarchy on the Canada tour. And he won an acco-lade from the Canadian people.

When he drove in from the Ottawa airport, wearing the uni-form of Marshal of the Royal Air Force with the blue sash of the Garter, the crowds again lined the streets to greet him. From the moment he reached Government House, however, protocol was limited. Three days afterward he opened the Empire Games in Vancouver, after having flown across the Dominion and toured the Chalk River atomic plant.

But it was when he turned northward that the tour first caught my imagination, as I think it did that of the world. He visited Kitimat in the British Columbia backwoods, where a new town-ship had arisen around the world's largest aluminum smelter.

These were developments and communities that had not existed a few years before; they had grown out of the wilderness, and now, visiting them, Philip reminded me more than ever of the boy exploring to the farthest depths of the woods. And when he flew, as the Queen's husband, across the untrodden Canadian desert to bustling, new places like Whitehorse, Port Radium, Yellowknife and Coppermine, one felt that real life had become stranger than fiction.

When I read that he had seen the cabin of Dangerous Dan McGrew in Whitehorse, I felt that I needed a picture postcard to make sure it was real.

Philip saw the northern Rockies blanketed in August snow; he glimpsed the thin ribbon of the Alaskan highway and went aboard one of the Yukon paddle steamers of the gold-rush days.

I think that he had a sense of unreality himself as he stood in the old-fashioned wheelhouse with the captain, sailing the Yukon River in the evening sunlight. A loudspeaker burst into "Cruising Down the River on a Sunday Afternoon," and Philip laughed. "Now I don't believe it!"

Moose was on the menu that night, needless to say. Adding his personal touch to the local atmosphere, Philip wore sticking plaster, the mark of the north, as if he had been scrapping with miners or lumberjacks. (The explanation was more humdrum, for he had scraped his nose by diving into the shallow end of a swimming pool back in Vancouver.)

The next day, he flew on: to Fort Nelson, where his party transferred to amphibious planes, to Fort Simpson, the old frontier headquarters of the Hudson's Bay Company in the fur-trading Mackenzie River district, where he met Indians, trappers and prospectors; and that evening the floats of his plane lapped down on Great Bear Lake for his visit to Port Radium.

As the Duke came ashore, the thirty-five children of the community drew up to greet him at the foot of the shale cliffs.

He was impressed by the strange loneliness of the area. Great Bear Lake is icebound nine months of the year and the nearest highway is seven hundred miles to the south. Apart from a few Indians and Eskimos, practically the only inhabitants of the vast area were the four hundred people of the mining settlement. He stayed that night in a white clapboard guesthouse and, after a modest supper, he took advantage of the long Arctic day to inspect the mine, descending more than twelve hundred feet to the levels where the radium is found.

The Arctic Circle was only thirty miles to the north and

Philip crossed it next morning. He was the first member of the Royal Family ever to do so. Flying over the bleak tundra, including the well-named Desolate Lakes and the September Mountains, his next objective was Coppermine.

He met at Coppermine a young Mountie who covers a beat of three thousand square miles by dogsled; he conversed with members of the Eskimo community through an interpreter; he visited a Hudson's Bay Company store and lunched on caribou steak and Arctic charr, the fish that white visitors know as Eskimo trout.

This was the northernmost point of his trip. After a two-hour stay he flew south again to Yellowknife, carrying a R.C.A.F. certificate that, by crossing the Arctic Circle that day, he had become "an airborne iceworm of an initial degree."

Yellowknife turned out to meet him with the lusty welcome of a town of gold miners and fishermen. There were more mines to inspect, and, from the basement of a timberman's home, Philip spoke over a network of amateur radio stations to the most isolated homesteads in the Canadian North. "Nobody could think of any reason why I should not come and have a look," he told his listeners. "So here I am."

At an evening barbecue on the beach the Duke lined up with the rest for his plate of bison-meat sandwiches. As the light faded, his personal standard fluttered above the two-story hotel and from his bedroom, he could hear the roaring business being done in the coffee room and bar. It was all very much what Philip expected; he was as far "out of this world" as it was possible for him to be. The next day, to satisfy his love of novelty, he drove in an armored Otter to Fort Churchill, the Canadian-American military base.

After some preliminary instruction, he took the amphibious

vehicle himself over the tundra and through brush, lakes and marshland.

It was later explained to him that the children at Churchill were accustomed to khaki-clad visitors and had been promised something special. "I quite understand," he said—and thus the little two-hundred-house settlement later witnessed the sight of the Duke of Edinburgh, in full Field Marshal's uniform, driving a jeep!

Before flying to Quebec City, he was presented with two polar-bear skins for Charles and Anne. "They're bound to get enormous fun out of them," he promised. He had already stored in the plane a boy-sized Arctic trapper's kit, Indian tunics, a toy sled and other gifts for his children.

This was a trip, indeed, from which Philip returned, filled with enthralling stories to tell his son. He sailed home in the *Britannia*, which he had met at Goose Bay, and boarded from an inlet scarcely on the map a dozen years before, that now adjoined an enormous airfield.

From that utterly transformed loneliness he next stepped ashore for an official welcome at Aberdeen. He then drove his own car to Balmoral, where his wife and children could not have been waiting more expectantly if he were returning from Mars.

Chapter 14

⋄ Philip and Son

1

ONCE, MANY years ago, when Philip and I were exchanging plans for the future and talking about the need of jobs for modern royalty, I asked him what he would like his children to be, if he had any.

"If I have a son," he said, "I'd like him to be a sailor. If I have a daughter, maybe she could become Queen."

We laughed and it turned into a joke at the time. Yet it seems strange that the wish should not only parallel what later happened to Philip and Elizabeth but, formulated casually, should be the basis of ideas Philip still holds for Prince Charles, Princess Anne and the new-born boy.

When he came home in August 1954, the royal couple hoped

that the year ahead, up to their planned State visit to Norway in June 1955, could be devoted to family life and home affairs.

Though it proved to be a period of the usual, intense public activity for Philip from a Commonwealth Industrial Study Conference to the State visit of the Emperor of Ethiopia, to the introduction of informal dinners (which have since become famous) for persons in art, science, commerce and industry and much more, it was also a breathing spell spent in England during which he could play a bigger role in Prince Charles's life.

He never felt in his own boyhood that there had been too many uncles. But he was aware that he never saw enough of his father. He wanted very much to avoid this unhappy circumstance with Charles and to make sure that the Prince had the necessary fatherly instruction and companionship.

Philip gave his son his first swimming lesson, set him astride his first pony, gave him his first miniature cricket bat and his first flip in a speedboat. He took him shooting in Norfolk and sailing in rough weather, at an age when many boys would still be in the charge of their nannies.

But Philip had also tempered his affection wisely by the thought that Charles must shape a life of his own.

Nothing altered his early conviction that the boy's proper education should be the same as that of an ordinary youngster, mixing with boys his own age, through kindergarten, prep school and at a public school.

It has been frequently said that this choice was his own, since Charles's education is the Duke of Edinburgh's prerogative, but Philip, I know, ironed out every detail in complete consultation with the Queen. There had never been any difference of opinion between them about it.

"I think people will have sense enough to give them a break," he said to me once when talking of plans. He and Elizabeth had hoped that, if an appeal was made to spare the children the embarrassment of constant publicity, both Charles and Anne could move about London like other youngsters.

To this extent, I am afraid, the parents have become disillusioned. When Charles first went to school and happened to join in a small-boy soccer match, one photographer was not above pushing his camera through the railings and taking telescopic shots that were all duly published.

The timing of the boy's schooling caused Philip a problem. Ultimately, when Charles went to special prep school in Chelsea at the age of eight a number of questions arose. Should he take part in the school play? Should he learn to box? Should he have school milk?

Though again Philip and Elizabeth indicated that he should be treated the same as the other boys, it proved impossible. People would wait on the pavement to see Charles come out, and the school sports demonstration received the press coverage of a national event.

After six months, when Charles transferred to Cheam, publicity precautions were drastically tightened. It was the first time an heir to the British throne had ever attended an ordinary prep school. A school letter was sent to the parents: "We trust that everything will proceed in the quiet way to which we are accustomed and we know we can count on your help."

Which school for the future? Philip has been extraordinarily good at keeping his own counsel but he has perhaps indicated the direction of his thoughts by his continued interest in Gordonstoun, the sailor's training ground.

It will not be enough for the Prince of Wales to join games with the sons of the non-royal rich. One day I am sure he will mix, as his father did, with the sons of miners and shopkeepers, factory workers and fishermen.

2

With the many opportunities for his son's company Philip thoroughly enjoyed the chief recreational holiday of 1955, the cruise in the *Britannia* with the children and Elizabeth.

They went to the western coasts of Britain and around the northern coast of Scotland to Aberdeen. When they landed for a beach picnic at Lindsway Bay near Milford Haven, Charles, the future Prince of Wales, stepped onto Welsh soil for the first time.

Philip had fun taking both the children in a speedboat, making quite a spectacular series of sharp turns, flinging up spray, and Charles whooped for more.

There were the usual pleasures of deck hockey, sun-bathing and swimming. Anne was learning how to swim and, showing no fear, was fast catching up with her brother.

Into this holiday the Queen and Prince Philip sandwiched an official three-day tour of western Wales, official visits to the Isle of Man and points in Scotland, and they reached Balmoral in time for Anne's fifth birthday.

Altogether, the cruise and later Balmoral stay was a most restful period in a dynamic year that embraced Philip's visit to Malta for Fleet exercises and, of course, the State visit to Norway in June, also undertaken in the *Britannia*.

Earlier, Aunt Alice had celebrated her seventieth birthday and Philip flew with Uncle Dickie from London for a family party at Salem. It was one of the happiest of occasions; Philip encountered nothing short of twelve nephews and nieces, and I think it was under these birthday auspices that he first had a hint of the budding romance between his niece, Princess Margarita of Baden, and my brother-in-law, Prince Tomislav.

A month later, his oldest sister, Princess Margarita, had her silver wedding anniversary and family rejoicing continued, now within the walls of Schloss Langenburg. This time, Philip flew his own plane to Stuttgart while Elizabeth attended the horse trials at Badminton, a typical instance of how these two sensibly divided time—and still do—for each other's interests. (From time to time of course Philip's sisters stay at Buckingham Palace, and Philip pays a weekend return visit when he can manage it, which proves to be an average of once or so a year.)

To help such jaunts and speed his public schedules, Philip mastered the helicopter that summer. After a week of lessons with Lieutenant Commander Max Simpson, he soloed.

When he began taking off and landing on the grounds of Buckingham Palace, prudent officials made sure that the resident doctor had a key to the Palace gardens just in case.

Historians will one day say that Philip pioneered the helicopter: he was so enthusiastic that both Aunt Elizabeth (the Queen Mother) and Princess Margaret were persuaded to try the aircraft, and Margaret used one for her tour in Germany that summer.

He went by helicopter to the Cowes regatta, flying low over the crowd, for a modern royal arrival. To open a playing field near London he cruised the ninety-minute road journey in a third the time. A controversy arose, however, when Philip began flying jet planes, and the drybones, as usual, had their say about the "hazards to a life precious both to the nation and the Queen."

As my pen charts Philip's activities in 1955, one finds him dining at the Institute of Naval Architects, at an anniversary dinner of chartered accountants, the guest of honor at the Burman service reunion, touring a new town or visiting a new oil refinery, blending familiar skeins of duty.

And one might add that his famous presidential address to

the British Association for the Advancement of Science was echoed when he spoke before the conference of European University Rectors and Vice-Chancellors at Cambridge and made one of his more striking personal declarations.

"I am not a graduate of any university," he said. "I am not a humanist or a scientist and, oddly enough, I don't regret it. I owe my allegiance to another of the world's few really great fraternities, the fraternity of the sea."

Chapter 15

From the Tropics to the Antarctic

1

NIGERIA RANKED as Britain's largest colony and protectorate and, potentially, the richest state in all of Africa. Yet it had never before been visited by a reigning British sovereign. So from the many, always-waiting invitations, Philip and Elizabeth selected it as the starting point of their next tour.

Its thirty-five million people were in the turmoil that accompanies the drive to self-determination. Only recently, like the people of Ghana, they had voted for complete independence within the Commonwealth. But Nigeria faced many difficulties in unifying herself under her own government, and the royal visit was intended to act as an important influence in bringing together the differing regions, tribes and creeds.

Though the appointment of two Nigerian equerries to the

Royal Household, the first colored men to serve in Buckingham Palace, was not Philip's original idea, it seems to have sprung from his powerful faith in the monarchy as the cement of the Commonwealth. Equally inspiring understanding was generated by the Queen.

The only precedent for one great ceremony of the tour, the Durbar, was forty years back when King George V and Queen Mary visited Delhi, India. The details of the Delhi Durbar were not of much help in planning for Nigeria. Royal salutes of one hundred one guns and a King's and Emperor's encampment of forty thousand tents belonged to another age.

But Elizabeth borrowed one gesture from it. When she was to appear at the Nigerian Durbar at Kaduna, at 9:30 in the morning, she planned to wear a full-length evening dress with a diamond tiara. The dress would match the splendor of the Durbar, just as her grandmother, my Aunt May, had done with her dress at Delhi to the awe of that assemblage.

Much new pomp and color was, of course, dictated by the unsophisticated customs of the country and its desire to please. Some embellishments that have been criticized, the gold-plated— or was it gold-painted?—wheels of the royal train, the lush carpets and costly air-conditioning of the Queen's lodgings, were in fact the ideas of the Nigerian Government.

Philip studied the practical as well as ceremonial details of the itinerary. He foresaw the need to give Elizabeth some shade in the equatorial sun. He had Norman Hartnell design a crown-topped canopy, a square of gilded aluminum, draped with light-weight velvet that could be carried about or used as a saluting base. This festive and modern accessory proved highly successful.

Philip also visualized the thousands who would crowd around at a garden party without hope of getting a glimpse of the Queen.

To many of them an emblem of Elizabeth's presence would be satisfying to see.

So a polished shaft was designed and constructed, topped by a silver crown and lion, to carry a royal standard, and a tall Nigerian orderly was appointed standard-bearer to follow the Queen as she moved through the people. This was indeed tribute to Philip's sense of pageantry.

On a wintry London afternoon, hundreds of Nigerian students, dressed in brilliantly colorful robes, gave the royal couple a resounding send-off at the airport. It was so heart-warming that Philip radioed back the Queen's thanks from the plane, a message that in turn warmed Nigerian hearts.

After touching down at Tripoli, they flew across the Sahara for Nigeria. Together, in the plane, they polished the speeches Elizabeth would give. Lord Altrincham chose, that year, to criticize the Queen's talks; he either overlooked or willfully ignored her words on this trip.

To open an Appeal Court, she was to say: "In our Commonwealth, the rule of law is maintained and all men are equal in the eyes of the law." And she told a mighty gathering of warriors and chieftains: "This great concourse . . . has brought home to me the respect you have for your ancient traditions. I, too, respect those traditions and hope that in a rapidly changing world you will maintain all that is good in them."

At Lagos, before the travelers were welcomed there onto African soil, the Oba, or heriditary ruler, had ordered his medicine man to make powerful ju-ju for a quick shower to clear the air, and lo, rain fell in the dry season for thirty-five minutes. This exemplified the blend of paganism, progress and good luck that became the keynote of the tour.

The swamplands of Nigeria had been the white man's grave, a gateway of darkest Africa. Now Philip found the country throbbing with vitality and adventure, a new world in the making.

The main route of the tour, formed by bush-hopping steps, went northward from Lagos on the Atlantic Coast, over the forests, to Moslem Nigeria at the edge of the Sahara, and then back again.

When they made a stop, it was noticeable from the first that the Queen continually left the white residents to talk to native Nigerians. Both Elizabeth and Philip tried to break through race and custom barriers, almost to demonstrate to Nigerians the way one could overcome the obstacles obstructing national unity.

When Elizabeth decorated the wife of a village blacksmith—the first Moslem woman in Nigeria to be so honored—and Philip engaged her in personal conversation, years of built-up prejudice were negated.

In a mining village the couple visited, all the women remained in their beehive huts, while the menfolk lined the roads for the royal show. Philip noticed the all-male element and guessed the difficulties. A few minutes later a woman in a hut heard a voice at the door. Philip was asking, "May I come in?"

I know how easy it is to think up such gestures that are unconventional, yet how difficult it is to carry them through with conviction. Philip was so fearless, however that throughout Nigeria he set aright many situations that others would have been flustered by or would have ignored.

At Ibadan, the largest native city in Nigeria, university students had threatened to boycott the visit because, it seems, they were dissatisfied about their representation at the address ceremony. Philip made a point of talking to one of the groups of students. "And are the boys behaving themselves?" he asked a young girl student. The reply was lost in the men students' burst of laughter.

Philip knew that he would encounter garish color, fantastic antiquity and barbaric rites contrasting with modern change. Even so, he was unprepared for the exotic spectacles staged in honor of the Queen and himself.

For instance, on the program of the tour it was announced that the Queen would "take the salute, on the race-course, of gentlemen representing the whole of the Northern Region."

This "salute" turned out to be a cavalcade of eight thousand magnificent chiefs, emirs and warriors clad in rainbow-hued medieval splendor, that concluded in a charge of fierce horsemen toward the royal dais. A "display of dancing" proved unexpectedly to be a rout of ten thousand whirling people, masked and painted, some of them mounted on stilts twelve feet high.

A "short visit to Port Harcourt" resulted in a race of giant war canoes, each manned by ninety men, the jangle of native bells and drums only drowned by ceremonial salvos from brass cannon of incredible age.

There were men dancers in beads and loincloths, women dancers in hooped skirts with bells on their legs, warrior dancers who juggled huge axes, and dancers in black goatskins and iron anklets who stamped out ritual steps against evil spirits.

Interspersed with these spectacles were visits to hospitals, colleges and mines, and side trips that took Elizabeth and Philip through palm-oil plantations to new towns. A fast-growing land was flexing its muscles for the Queen.

On one occasion, a Nigerian ex-soldier appeared at the side of the open car so unexpectedly that Philip jumped. The man wanted only to thrust a petition into his hands. But the Nigerian's glaring eyes and the responsive roar of horror from the crowd served to exemplify the frightening passion and energy of the country.

There was an incident of a different kind when the couple went to a leper settlement, the first ever visited by members of the Royal Family, and a blind leper, at the sound of their approach, stepped forward to make an impromptu speech of welcome. Shaking his hand and thanking him, Philip set aside centuries of Nigeria's own fears.

It was here that Elizabeth and Philip adopted two children, a girl and a boy. Most people only know of Charles, Anne and Andrew, but Nigeria knows they have a family of five.

2

Homeward bound, the royal plane briefly stopped at Kano, a great outpost on the edge of the Sahara. Less than a century and a half before, no white man had ever seen the mud-walled city though it had an African history of a thousand years.

Turbaned Moslem horsemen, wearing heirloom armor made at the time of the Crusades, formed a guard of honor. In petunia satin and purple and silver headdress, the Emirs of Kano, Gumel, Kazure and Hadeija came to greet and pay homage to the Queen and her husband, while masked Tuaregs watched in the crowds.

I venture to think this romantic. I was so interested at the time that I checked on the map and discovered that Kano is not far, as the plane flies, from Timbuktoo. I remember reflecting that if we, in the family, were losing our sense of wonder at all the bizarre things happening to Philip, we had certainly been premature.

To cap the changes of scene my cousin made, barely a fortnight later he was back in the Mediterranean, attending Fleet exercises. This time, seven years away from his snug little bunk on the *Chequers*, he was aboard the *Britannia*.

I heard that he had been anxious for Elizabeth to enjoy one of the discoveries of his naval days—the sunshine and unspoiled atmosphere of Corsica.

When she joined the *Britannia* and they sailed through the Straits of Bonifacio, unhappily they met biting wind and rain. The weather improved a day or two later but then press interest in the visitors became so great that the hoped-for opportunity of undisturbed sight-seeing never arrived.

Afterward, Philip returned to as busy a six months as any he had ever spent. Once again they toured, visited and camped out nights in the royal train: a round of over three hundred engagements ranging from the foundation ceremony of the new Coventry Cathedral to tea with Nikita Khrushchev, the Russian Premier, at Windsor Castle.

June found the Queen and Philip back aboard the *Britannia* for the State visit to Sweden, and I heard quite a bit about this from my Swedish cousins.

The Royal Family in Sweden is usually able to move about without too much commotion; yet, it was agreed, Elizabeth's and Philip's visit was sensational.

Queen Olga of Sweden is, of course, Philip's aunt. The Swedish crowds demonstrated almost as much affection for him, a royal nephew, as they did for Elizabeth as visiting Queen.

Their arrival coincided with the Olympic Games equestrian events; they trudged through the mud to watch the endurance tests of the horsemen and enjoyed themselves thoroughly.

Philip is often supposed, quite wrongly, to have no interest in horses, apart from polo ponies. In reality, besides his presidential appointments, he belongs to several riding and racing clubs and has been a member of the Royal Naval Saddle Club and the Jockey Club from the years before his marriage.

Moreover, as for attending the trials, he was due to open the 1956 Olympic Games in Melbourne, Australia, in October, and the Swedes regarded his presence in Stockholm as a necessary prerequisite.

The visit to Sweden and a cruise to the western isles of Scotland were minor movements in the graph of royal travel, but Nigeria was no sooner over than nearly every day brought Philip a fresh invitation or request to include in the schedule of his coming world tour.

It was a journey planned at first with a comparatively simple motive, the opening of the Olympic Games. But it began to develop into a tour of astonishing length, and it was destined to take Philip on a thirty-eight-thousand-mile odyssey to some of the smallest and most remote communities under the British Crown.

The world tour was to be shorn of formality, just close companions aboard the *Britannia*, and a reasonable balance was to be struck, perhaps for the first time on a royal trip, between hard work and real holidaying.

When Philip left London on October 15, his wife and children and his youngest sister, Sophie, saw him off at London airport. He traveled with Lieutenant Commander Michael Parker, his private secretary; Squadron Leader Henry Chinnery, his equerry; Viscount Cilcennin, former First Lord of the Admiralty; and Dr. Wold Breitling, a friend of Michael Parker's. But at Mombasa, where the royal yacht waited for them, a difficulty remained to be settled before the journey could begin its carefree course.

This was to be Michael's last tour as private secretary. The genial Australian, facing an impasse in his private affairs, had in fact handed in his resignation and Philip had regretfully accepted it. A long friendship had reached the turning point.

The two had met originally as first lieutenants on destroyer patrols in the North Sea; and their friendship was maintained after the war when Michael began a business career in London.

One of Philip's implicit problems has always been to recruit a staff personal to himself and out of the mainstream of traditional courtiers. In 1949 he had offered his astonished friend the post of equerry and for nearly nine years the two had been practically inseparable.

The breakdown of Parker's marriage had brought disruption. Clearly the high standard that made the Court maintain the Ascot royal-enclosure ban upon the guilty parties to divorce could allow no distinctions at the Palace, and Michael's resignation was unavoidable.

In his difficulty, Philip turned back to Gordonstoun and re-membered James Orr, who had preceded him a year or two earlier at the school as head boy. Among other activities, Orr was now a chief inspector with the Kenya Police Reserve, so Philip suggested that they meet together in Mombasa. The out-come was successful.

Mr. Orr duly succeeded at Buckingham Palace. Whatever happened in public, however, Philip's friendship with Michael certainly continued. My husband and I had a reassuring glimpse of this the following year at Tommy's wedding (the wedding of my brother-in-law, Prince Tomislav of Yugoslavia, to Princess Margarita of Baden, Philip's niece). It was a real family party. Philip was of course one of the foremost guests and with him, ebullient as ever, was Michael Parker.

3

From the Seychelle Islands, claimed to be the original Garden of Eden, the Queen heard that all was well. From Colombo she heard that the Ceylon Yacht Club had arranged some fine sail-ing, and soon the photographs began to pour in from the tiny Malayan isle of Langkawi, from Penang and Kuala Lumpur.

The thunderstorms Philip encountered made him recall his

first sea days as a midshipman. But, in less than a month after leaving London, he and his party were in Papua, savoring new experience.

Native chieftains and clay-masked women accorded them a vociferous welcome; Girl Scouts, wearing only skirts and ties, paraded before them and a thousand New Guinea warriors broke ranks and ran during a tropical downpour for fear the rain would spoil their war paint.

At Lae, also in New Guinea, Philip heard from the District Commissioner that his native name was "Number-One-Fellah-Belong-Missus-Queen," an honorific he later delightedly repeated to British television viewers.

Then there were the drums and dancers of Gabensis and Rabaul. At Manus the deep-chested Pacific islanders staged a magnificent display in war canoes, dancing their greetings (while afloat) and even demonstrating pottery making, complete with a kiln, while skimming the surf.

Tours were made, of course, to rubber plantations, timber mills, plywood factories and copra sheds but the visits derived intrinsic interest rather than tiresome royal obligation. "Almost everywhere I went was new and fascinating," Philip reported.

Arriving by air at Darwin, in North Australia, the party lost no time driving out to the open-cut uranium mine at Rum Jungle. "[It] gave us an impression of the flat and unending bush," they noted.

That night, for a rare adventure, Philip joined a crocodile hunt through the swampy creeks of the Darwin foreshore. His host had had a narrow escape only a few days before, after falling overboard while trying to harpoon a twelve-foot "croc." In the searching headlight of their boat, the creatures' eyes burned like cigarette ends. But Philip was able to report to his wife that he had bagged a lashing six-footer.

He had asked for informality and he got it as he flew in sweltering heat to an outback cattle station, visited the town called Alice, and attended a memorable steak barbecue there at sundown.

A few days later, the lonely wilderness of Australia gave way to the crowded stadium in Melbourne, packed with one hundred twenty thousand spectators and four thousand athletes. Here Philip made his shortest recorded speech: "I declare open the Olympic Games of Melbourne, celebrating the sixteenth Olympiad of the modern era."

The Melbourne police were worried by a series of crank letters threatening Philip's life but fortunately nothing untoward occurred. The weekend was spent with old friends. Afterward, I think he particularly enjoyed a visit to the spectacular Snowy Mountains on an inspection of the gigantic hydro-electric system. A guest cottage had been prepared for him, in the workers' township, but the flowers and flags could not conceal that it was just two tiny prefab bungalows put end to end. Philip was asked to name his smallest royal residence. "Why not the Duke box?" he suggested with a twinkle. Then he compromised on "Edinburgh Castle."

By tightly scheduled air travel, he next returned to Melbourne to watch a section of the Games, and then flew on to Sydney, where the city turned out to accord him a spontaneous ticker-tape welcome.

The only dissident Sydney citizen, a man who twice tried to throw himself under Philip's car, shouting wild protests against royal ceremonies, simply timed his demonstration badly. It was the least pompous and least ceremonial royal parade ever.

The modern-minded Lord Mayor flew Philip over the city by helicopter to give him a view of new roads and playing fields. Then, back in Melbourne after two intensive days of municipal sight-seeing, Philip was televised in church—to be exact St. Paul's Cathedral—as he read the lesson.

Visiting the Olympiad village after the service, he arrived thirty minutes earlier than had been expected and was greeted by a riotous squad of cooks and waitresses rather than orderly ranks of athletes. But he passed the time inspecting the kitchens, I heard, until the official welcoming committee got there. It was to his taste.

He typically preferred to wander through the crowds of athletes, into the sauna bath and the hospital and living quarters, than to inspect officially, for he enjoyed keenly the informality and the sense of good fellowship.

Toward the end of this crowded week, the Lord Mayor conferred the Freedom of the City of Melbourne upon him. Though Elizabeth and Philip have the freedom of many cities, Philip notably became the *first* Freeman of Melbourne; it was the first time the city had ever bestowed the honor in her long history.

Meanwhile, the *Britannia* had gone ahead, and Philip left Melbourne by air on December 11 to pick her up in New Zealand, where another hectic week of welcome and tours ensued.

By now, at Philip's invitation, Mr. Edward Seago had joined the ship as an unofficial artist of the Antarctic leg of the tour, and with him was Sir Raymond Priestley, President of the British Association for the Advancement of Science, ranking, however, as a specialist in that he had been on Scott's expedition to the South Pole. Mr. Seago found Philip preparing for the Antarctic with characteristic thoroughness, studying a library full of special books that had been brought aboard.

At home the newspapers declaimed, "It will be the first time a member of the Royal Family has visited the geologists, surveyors and meteorologists who man scattered outposts of the Commonwealth at the bottom of the world."

But, while those resounding words were still in the typewriters, New Zealand youngsters were singing him a rock n' roll farewell of "See you later, alligator," and Philip (remembering his recent hunt) showed himself no square by shouting the retort, "In a while, crocodile."

Two days before Christmas, the *Britannia*, headed south, ran into her first snowstorm, and the oiler *Wave Chief* signalled the royal yacht, "In the event of encountering pack-ice suggest you take station astern of me and take advantage of my semi-strengthened bows." Philip accepted that invitation with celerity.

4

An enduring tradition is one of royalty's amazing inheritances. In the Falkland Islands Philip found relics of the visit of King George V as a midshipman during the cruise of the sailing ship *Bacchante* forty years before Philip and I had been born.

I am leaping a little ahead in my narrative and my excuse is that my imagination is stirred recalling the words of his Christmas Day broadcast from the Antarctic, "We are the solid facts beneath the words and phrases, we are the solid flesh-and-blood links which draw the Commonwealth under the Crown."

The *Bacchante* had drifted rudderless in a hurricane in those freezing waters owing to damage to the steering gear. Though the *Britannia* was less subject to such a breakdown, the seas were rough and water contaminated the fuel oil of the tanker ship *Wave Chief*, which necessitated loading of fresh oil in the middle of the castellated icebergs and patchy fog.

Before long, to quote an official report, "The Antarctic was playing up perfectly in the matter of local color. Icebergs and glaciers shone brilliantly under blue skies as if produced by technicolor."

Aboard ship, Philip suggested a beard competition, via notice on the bulletin board. The others in the crew accepted. Beards sprouted in every shade from black to brilliant red; the only clean-shaven men were Lord Cilcennin and Sir Raymond Priestley, who were soon appointed umpires.

On New Year's day, 1957, when Philip transferred to the research ship *John Biscoe* for his visit to the bases of Grahamland, he had already grown a considerable red stubble.

He had hoped to visit the advanced bases of the forthcoming Transantarctic Expedition, but no suitable icebreaker was available and he had to be content with going no farther south than Base W on Deception Island.

In eighteen months' time he had crossed both the Arctic and Antarctic Circles, not to mention three times over the Equator. Probably, after this background, his least-anticipated impression of the Antarctic was its *smell*: the revolting odor of the penguin rookeries, the halitosis of the elephant seals and the stench of the whale factories.

The beaches were littered with the white bones of whales, symbolic of slaughter accumulated from Moby Dick days. The dispatches home described Lord Cilcennin stoutly defending himself against the diving attacks of two enraged skua gulls with a rib bone of one of these whale skeletons.

Between the Falklands and South Georgia, the *Britannia* met three whale chasers at work in a sea obstructed by enormous icebergs. "The yacht chased the catcher as the catcher chased the whale," Philip wrote. "The whale turned and jinked and never allowed the gunner to get in a decent shot."

Formality was adopted briefly when Philip went ashore at

Port Stanley, the capital of the Falkland Islands, in full-dress uniform. Distinct informality returned that afternoon when he rode in a sailor's horse race on the local course and won in a new style of riding which might, he felt, have been hotly debated at home. During his stay, the Falklands held sheepdog trials and staged a farmer's luncheon, a football match and many other diverting affairs.

A week later, the *Britannia* arrived at Gough Island, having circumnavigated the world in one hundred thirty-five days, an event celebrated by the issue of an Antarctic "Red Nose Certificate," which Philip and Edward Seago had jointly designed, to every member of the ship's company.

In the deep South Atlantic, precipitous Gough Island proved to be uninhabited except by penguins, mice and four lonely South African meteorologists.

They reached Tristan da Cunha the following day, where a canvas-hulled longboat sailed through the rollers to meet the Prince on the yacht. Once again he was in full gold tabs as an Admiral of the Fleet, to demonstrate his respect for a tiny, lonely community. And with the familiar informality that heightened his visits, he took the longboat's tiller from the island pilot and skillfully landed the craft himself.

A short while later, the *Britannia* went two hundred fifty miles off her course to answer the call of an Argentine ship, whose first engineer was seriously ill with appendicitis. Dr. Breitling recommended an immediate operation, which involved transferring the sick man to the *Britannia* in a heavy sea. The appendix was removed, and the next day the *Britannia* landed the invalid at St. Helena.

St. Helena had four thousand people and many came to greet Philip. Touring around the Napoleonic Isle, he must have revived memories of the family stories told him years before by our Bonapartean relative, Aunt Marie.

At Ascension Island, he obligingly gazed at sea turtles, fruit gardens, and at volcanic ash heaps which, he said, reminded him of the scene he might see if he visited the moon. But he had barely time to shake his head in wonder, for he was soon at the little colony of Gambia, the last British landfall of the tour.

Gambia is the smallest of all British African possessions and, as Philip stepped ashore, a gun salute was suitably fired by a troop of Boy Scouts. Earlier, he had personally brought the royal yacht into Bathhurst but had not been recognized, a bearded young man in white shirt and shorts, as he waved at the quay. Now as he perched on the hood of a touring car for the official procession, the beaming Gambians are reported to have yelled, "Welcome Duke and Jesus keep you for the Queen." The greeting seems even stranger when one reflects that the majority of Gambians are Moslems.

Philip found the main street an avenue of spears and shields, of Fula women with curling black horns in their hair and tall women from nomadic Mauretania in robes of scarlet, yellow and peanut.

The welcome in Bathurst and Sankwia was no less enthusiastic than the welcome to the Seychelles four months earlier. At the Recreation Ground the program of native dances included the novelty of a dancing camel, and the Wolaf women presented Philip with sixty versions of himself whirling and cavorting, his portrait printed lifesize on their costumes.

Later, at Philip's request, one of the thrills enjoyed in northern Australia was repeated with a crocodile hunt organized on the Gambia River.

This led to an encounter with the Rasputin of crocodiles, a monster shot four times through the head by Michael Parker and given the coup de grâce by Philip. It was hauled aboard the hunting boat only to come to life again "with snarlings and thrashings," to everyone's alarm, until a local villager finally killed it with a knife.

Philip shortly departed on the run home. On February 1, the great beard competition ended; the prize for the bushiest—a bottle of shaving lotion—went to a tough petty officer, and the prize for the most colorful went to a ship's musician, concealed behind a mat of violent carrot. Other awards were made for the most distinguished, the most handsome, and "the one that didn't quite." The impresario of the contest was not eligible for a prize.

Chapter 16

◆ Tagus and Ticker Tape

1

Two WEEKS away from the public eye, free of cameramen and correspondents, had been intended for Philip in the final phase of his around the world tour.

After leaving Gambia on January 31 he was not due to meet the Queen until she arrived in Lisbon, in readiness for their State visit to Portugal, on February 16.

He envisaged a lazy interlude on the beaches of two outlying islands in the Canaries, but these coasts proved unsuitable for swimming or sun-bathing. So he sailed to Gibraltar on February 6, earlier than he had expected.

As in previous years, he was scheduled to participate in Gibraltar naval exercises, inspect units of the Home Fleet and fly with the R.A.F. Coastal Command, but during the past months the Suez crisis had left the Mediterranean in such a ferment that it was thought best to cancel his appearances and make his visit "unofficial."

This action led, however, to an unanticipated fusillade of rumor, so wide of the mark that it makes me angry to write of it. Philip's unofficial stopover at Gib was interpreted, in some newspapers, as unwillingness to return to his wife in London.

The news of Michael Parker's resignation broke at the same time, and the American front pages bubbled with stories of a rift between the royal couple. Naturally, the Palace press attaché, on being questioned, issued a denial, but he only added fuel to the fire.

It was galling to Philip to return from a tour of duty, during which he had worked harder to know the British Commonwealth than any other man and find himself facing this charge of disloyalty.

He had hoped that his journey could highlight the Commonwealth as a family of nations "sticking together not by force but because we like each other" and instead he found that moral practically smothered in soap opera.

In private, Philip and Elizabeth had planned their reunion in Lisbon with an ardent longing that Peter and I could well understand.

After nearly ten years of marriage, a couple needs to contrive a romantic new meeting, and the fatherly President Lopes of Portugal was their understanding host.

It was agreed weeks beforehand that Philip would meet Elizabeth as she arrived by plane at a Portuguese airfield, and whisk her away for a weekend aboard the *Britannia* before they began the four-day State visit.

I think we all knew that the columnists, having cooked up a quarrel, would serve the reunion hot from the griddle: it was the longest separation husband and wife had endured.

But as I read of the "radiantly happy Queen" and "the Duke smudged with lipstick," I confess I was particularly baffled by the report that he was wearing a tie ornamented with hearts. Philip simply couldn't be playing up so obviously, I told myself, and it turned out that much had been made of a triviality.

A valet happened to select a regimental tie presented to Philip in New Zealand. It was a tie of the Hawkes Bay Regiment, and I suppose the valet vaguely thought it might be nice for the Duke to wear a tie he hadn't had when he went away. It was cheerfully ornamented with small stags' heads worked in gold and, from a distance, they resembled hearts.

But, if I had been given the opportunity at the time, I imagine I could quickly have dispelled the rift rumors simply by telling something I knew.

In his hotel suite in Auckland, New Zealand, Philip had noticed a photograph of the Halliday portrait of the Queen and he liked it so much that he took it down from the wall, then and there, to put in his suitcase and take with him to the Antarctic. This was scarcely the gesture of someone running away from marriage.

Happily, Elizabeth and Philip have never allowed themselves to be affronted by misrepresentation, and they enjoyed infectiously the excitement of the Portuguese welcome.

Everything went with a wonderful swing from the moment eighty red-coated oarsmen rowed them from the *Britannia* across the Tagus in the gilded royal barge. This was only the second time that ancient craft had been used since the visit of King Edward VII in 1903.

In the decorated avenues and squares the cheers of tens of thousands seemed to Philip's trained ear to have that wistful fervor he had noted before in countries without a monarchy.

Perhaps, though, it was the traditional courtesy of the Portuguese people, everywhere flying the Union Jack (right way up with astonishing correctness) and decking windows and balconies with bed covers to add to the festiveness.

He and the Queen responded in kind, nowhere more than on their last official function in Oporto when they unexpectedly left the royal car, with its rather dark interior, and commandeered a police bus from photographers.

While the cameramen climbed into the car with the Royal Standard, Elizabeth and Philip clambered into the high back seat of the open bus where they could be seen by everyone. Considerations of safety, of which they are so often reminded, were set aside. And then down came the flowers, thrown from balconies and pavements and housetops until the bus was full of blossoms and Philip himself could scoop them up by the armful to toss. Once in a while, even a Queen can dream of a fiesta of welcome achieved with utter perfection and I think Oporto supplied it.

2

Back in London Uncle Dickie Mountbatten and Edwina gave a theater party for the returned travelers. They went to see the two-man show, *At the Drop of a Hat*, and joined heartily in the "Hippopotamus Song" with its refrain, "Mud, mud, glorious mud. . . . Nothing quite like it for cooling the blood." I imagine Philip had cause to find the words running through his head afterward with a droll sense of private significance.

Publicly, he tried to distil his motive in a speech he gave at a Mansion House luncheon. "I believe that there are some things for which it is worth while making some personal sacrifices," he said. "I believe that the British Commonwealth is one of those things, and I am for one prepared to sacrifice a good deal if by so doing I can advance its well-being by even a small degree."

The audience responded vociferously. And the Queen added her own recognition by preparing the announcement, "The Queen has been pleased . . . to give and grant unto H.R.H. the Duke of Edinburgh the style and titular dignity of a Prince of the United Kingdom. The Queen has been pleased to declare her will and pleasure that the Duke of Edinburgh shall henceforth be known as His Royal Highness the Prince Philip, Duke of Edinburgh."

Thus Philip again became a royal prince, after nearly ten years of royal dukedom. He had been born a prince, he had relinquished his titles, and he had been a commoner before being raised to a duke.

The news crystallized for me in a story told by an old friend of mine on the Côte d'Azur. When Philip was in his twenties, the older man had deferred to him as a Prince of Greece and Denmark. But when Philip became a commoner and visited the Riviera, he refused to accept the man's deference.

"No, General," he explained. "I'm now plain Lieutenant Mountbatten and so I defer to you."

Time passed. When Philip next paid a visit to Monte Carlo he was Duke of Edinburgh; so once again the punctilious general deferred to him and this time Philip accepted.

The success of his world tour brought Philip fuller honor than title, its essence summed up in the compliments of the Lord Mayor of London in proposing Philip's health: "You cannot please all people all the time. You do not please the half-hearted, the defeatists, the players for safety. But you delight and thrill the eager, the energetic and the brave, the men and women who look to the future."

Philip was still only thirty-five. Among the innovations of the year in 1957 was the illustrated lecture about his trip that he

233

gave at the Royal Festival Hall to eighteen hundred children. The audience was chosen impartially from two hundred secondary schools, nine children from each school. The talk was such a success that he repeated a forty-minute version afterward on television, and though nominally on a Children's Hour program, his lecture attracted a vast adult audience.

It led in turn to the more ambitious venture of Philip's inauguration of the International Geophysical Year, as commentator in a seventy-five-minute "prime time" program. Ostensibly, he headed the proceedings by his office as Senior Fellow of the Royal Society, but we all sensed that he felt challenged by a new world to conquer in the dimension of television and that he eagerly wanted to make his conquest absolute.

His commentary was an exposition of geophysical science in probing the secrets of space and he carried it off brilliantly, supervising the script, linking a series of films and outside broadcasts, and moving from point to point on the elaborate set to handle full-size replicas of satellite rockets and models of the globe.

The rehearsals were fitted into the packed routine of his official day. I realized how hard he was working when I heard that he went to the studio in the morning, broke off to attend a military display in the afternoon and went back in the evening, prepared to rehearse through midnight.

That April saw the State visit of Elizabeth and Philip to Paris staged with greater splendor than perhaps any royal occasion since the war. Peter and I, living on the Côte d'Azur, felt the enthusiasm rolling across France like a tide.

I now found myself wishing, as I did often, that Philip had not become so reticent and self-contained. I should like to have known how he felt as he rode in the presidential car, accorded the fullest honors of France.

Aware that the television cameras would be trained on her

more fully than at any time since the Coronation, Elizabeth was fretting lest she should fall short of the fantastically high standards of perfection that she always set herself. Yet she need not have worried. She was at the zenith of the beauty of her twenties and Philip was very proud of her.

It is recorded that when she appeared on the floodlit balcony of the Opéra a half million people, massed in every radiating street, gave a sigh of admiration and pleasure.

The city of Paris had set itself to enhance the royal program with the utmost charm and taste.

Philip, usually so severely practical, said afterward that the night cruise along the illuminated banks of the Seine had been enchanting.

With exquisite artistry, Serge de Poligny had arranged a pageant of Parisian history along the floodlit quays as if the river banks were a panoramic stage: every oncoming bridge or turn of the river revealed a new tableau. Now there were vividly dressed groups of folk dancers, now courtly dancers of the reign of Henry IV, and then the spectacle of a flower market leaped in sudden and dazzling illumination from the darkness as the royal guests glided by. I can well understand their enthusiasm, and they told me later how sharply Philip savored the contrast between the glitter of that occasion and the solitudes he had visited earlier in the year.

The following month, the busy pair were off again. The trip to Denmark was their third State visit of the year and this time a note of comedy entered the ceremony.

My cousin, King Frederick of Denmark, is a great exponent of physical culture, exercising continually with heavy weights, barbells and so forth; but in his determination to be in fit condition for his guests, he had strained a muscle in his back. The sad result was that, while exchanging greetings or inspecting a guard of honor he was apt to double up in great pain. Nothing could be done but make light of it and so, for all Elizabeth's and Philip's concern, the visit was punctuated with frequent laughter.

It was, nonetheless, a full journey. The first day's schedule lasted fifteen hours, the second day thirteen (beginning with a visit to the Carlsberg brewery at 9:30 A.M.) and the third day fourteen hours.

The State dinner at Christiansborg Castle was the first occasion on which television cameras attended a royal banquet and the Eurovision link-up gave the speeches an audience of fifty million.

Philip did not have to speak; otherwise, I imagine he would have recalled that he had returned to the home of his forefathers. Indeed, if his grandfather, Prince George of Denmark, had not become King of Greece less than a hundred years before, Denmark might well have been Philip's own country today.

The bustle of the year continued after they bade farewell. The *Britannia*, in returning from Denmark, carried the Queen and Philip direct to a review of the Home Fleet at Invergordon. They visited R.A.F. airfields in Scotland and journeyed to Stratford-on-Avon and Yorkshire, apart from undertaking rigorous television rehearsals and preparing for the coming tour of North America.

Just at about this time I remember a friend earnestly asking me, "Is Philip doing too much, do you think?"

Talk got around that he was looking peaked and thin and he was reported to be increasingly irritable. On two occasions, in June and July that year, he was involved in minor car accidents which may have been symptoms of personal strain.

He was in some difficulty when, driving Elizabeth to Windsor one afternoon, he grazed an old car emerging from a side street. A witnessing crowd seemed to spring up from the pavement.

He discreetly had to take the blame and drive away as soon as possible. And only that lunchtime he had made an official speech about road safety.

I have known Philip to grumble, "It's just not my day!" His few other mishaps had occurred during the trying period of emergence into public life just before and after his marriage, and I believe that the summer of 1957 found Philip going through a phase of adjustment no less fundamental and critical.

He was being praised for having "streamlined the monarchy." Perhaps more than the Queen, he had indeed initiated many reforms in the court structure and he was sympathetic to every attempt to remove the anachronisms and absurdities from protocol.

He had set every member of the Royal Family traveling with a deepened sense of mission to the far ends of the earth, strengthening the links of Commonwealth, when once it had been a major event for royalty to visit a provincial town.

He had encouraged the Queen to replace the unnecessary, annual debutante presentation parties with larger Commonwealth garden parties at which guests from many walks of life could be entertained.

He had instituted weekly round-table luncheons with the Queen, drawing guests from all classes of society. Some of his changes were involuntary. When he installed the all-pervading intercom, it marked an end to centuries of message-carrying royal attendants. The new informality spread to the Queen's audiences with ambassadors and ministers (as, indeed, the informality of the age was bound to do), and it allowed television to broadcast events as ceremonious, yet important to the ordinary man, as the opening of Parliament.

It would be wrong to ascribe to Philip a personal responsibility for every new change in procedure. But he has always been realistic about reform, and to an extent his extrovert nature has made him its natural champion.

So Philip was riled to find angry but ignorant young men attacking "the royal round of gracious boredom, the protocol of ancient fatuity" months and even years after the last semblance of these hobgoblins had been swept from the palace.

It made him an "angry young man" himself when his wife's talents were in any way devalued. He was himself neither the nonentity described by Prince Albert, "shunning all attention, assuming no separate responsibility," nor was he a Svengali to the Queen's Trilby. The truth lay somewhere in between.

Philip could do whatever was in his power to foster the long tradition of the monarchy, yet ultimately he found himself walled within the customs of the unwritten constitution to which he and the Queen were prisoners.

Only to each other were Philip and Elizabeth ordinary people. Their own mothers sometimes had to observe the curtsey before the kiss on the cheek.

For a wider release—to let off steam, as Philip might put it— the Queen could turn to her thoroughbred race horses and her riding.

For Philip himself there were the absorptions of yachting and polo, both of them team sports yet demanding the utmost quickness and vigor of the individual.

Philip was at Cowes and Cowdray a good deal during the summer of 1957. He was a member of the Household Brigade Saddle Club and the Ham Polo Club as well as the Cowdray Club. He played with new tenacity and aggressiveness, and the Windsor Park team pushed through to the final of the Cowdray Park Gold Cup for the first time. Philip had two falls—one can imagine the headlines!—but was unhurt.

He made a trial gliding trip that summer too. He went up,

in Peter Scott's glider, in a cross wind that might have taken him from the Cotswolds to Scotland had anything more than a short flight been on schedule.

I particularly appreciated an occasion when he flew by helicopter from the royal yacht to pilot a glider during the national gliding championships, and then traveled on by helicopter to play polo. This was, one might say, "pure" Philip.

3

During the preparations for the 1957 North American visit, Philip edited a volume of his own speeches, sponsored an exhibition at St. James's Palace of the souvenirs of his Commonwealth-Antarctic tour and went through many impromptus. In one ceremony, he became a godfather within my husband's family, his charge being the baby daughter of Prince Andrea of Yugoslavia and Princess Christina of Hesse, who is, of course, Philip's niece.

The visit to Ottawa, Washington and New York was a new kind of royal tour in that, with receptions, banquets, drives, and inspections, all the usual elements of a much longer trip were present, but the exhausting program was crammed into a bare ten days.

Fresh from a Balmoral holiday, Elizabeth and Philip were unstinting with their time and energy. On the average, the tour allowed them only six hours' sleep in twenty-four.

Reports estimate that they shook ten thousand hands and were seen by some five million people along the parade routes. It was a great success, more pleasing to them both in that it helped repair Anglo-American relations that had been strained only a year before by the Suez crisis.

It was six years since Philip had first accompanied Elizabeth to Canada. Now when she went as Queen of that nation he was thoroughly practiced in his supporting role.

At their first function, a reception for newspapermen at Government House, Ottawa, held shortly after they stepped off the plane, a friend wrote me about Philip's skill in shaking hands with over five hundred correspondents an hour. Philip stopped every third person or so and asked, "Where are you from?" as if the papers for which they worked mattered vitally.

Elizabeth altered the question to "Who are you with?" and once had a nonplused reporter point to his friends and say, "I'm with them."

If, in the old days, kings and queens relied on pomp and panoply as well as their own personalities to make them larger than life, the task had now passed for good or ill to the forces of modern publicity.

Over three thousand reporters and photographers gave the 1957 visit coverage in Canada and the United States. Elizabeth appeared on Canadian-American television, and Philip encouraged her just out of camera range.

At her television debut, he contributed one of his private jokes, at just the right moment. "Tell the Queen to remember the wailing and gnashing of teeth!" he told the director as she was going on the air.

Mystified, the director did so. Elizabeth flashed a brilliant smile and, the next instant, her manner had just the right ease as she spoke to sixty million viewers.

With sc many press reports of events, I feel that I should really confine myself to describing unofficial incidents.

At the opening of the Canadian Parliament, for example, strong film lights blew all the fuses in the House barely five minutes before the royal carriage was due. The fuses were replaced and the lights went on again just fifty-five seconds before the

Queen and Philip arrived; they knew nothing about it when they entered.

The next day, shaking hands with thirteen hundred guests at a reception, Philip was warned to watch for ten Red Indian chiefs who would be in the line wearing mufti. Recognizing the Chief of the Six Nations, Philip asked the meaning of a button he wore in his lapel.

"Twenty-five years with the post office," the American Indian explained proudly.

It was noted with astonishment that Philip recognized many of the people he had met casually on his summer visit to Canada three years before.

In addition to the Queen's engagements, he separately received the Canadian members of his Oxford study conference and made a radio talk about the conference and some of its results. These interludes were all timed to the minute, of course. When the royal couple arrived in Jamestown, Virginia, for their first eight-hour program on American soil, the agenda clearly stipulated one joint rest period, ten minutes for the Queen— and five for Philip.

The visit to Jamestown was specially to commemorate the three hundred and fiftieth anniversary of the establishment of the first British colony in the New World, and Philip exercised great self-control when he was received by a comic opera guard of honor in Elizabethan costumes, bewigged with curls.

The columnist who felt that Philip "kept fury capped behind a handsome smile" may, however, have changed his mind when the Prince, in an interchange of university gifts, began genially, "I know it isn't Christmas but here are some more presents."

They spent the night at the Williamsburg Inn, their room adjoining a staircase awkwardly narrow for Elizabeth's ball gown, and early next morning flew to Washington where President

Dwight Eisenhower waited to welcome them at the airport.

Their tour included children's hospitals, receptions, art galleries, wreath laying and much more, a grand total of one hundred fourteen ceremonies in eighty-one hours; and bright new notes were added.

The crowds were more responsive than on the previous visit. The famous trip to a supermarket had the air of being completely impromptu, but I think that Philip discussed it with protocol officials well before.

Probably everyone knows the story of the little woman in front of the light bulb counter, trying to make up her mind whether she should buy one 100-watt bulb or two sixties. She looked up and there was the Queen.

On Philip's side there is the story, in more ironic vein, of the bland American husband whom he asked, "Doing the shopping?"

"I was," the man said, "until you interrupted."

An Australian was the senior Commonwealth representative in Washington and so it was protocol that the traditional return dinner to their host should be staged, the final night in Washington, in the Australian Embassy. It served both as a reminder to isolationists that the British Commonwealth never can be isolated and that the Queen was visiting Washington as the representative of many peoples. It was amusing to hear President Eisenhower's parting impression of Elizabeth as confided to a friend of mine, "She's a good girl. She's all right." As for Philip, the saying went around, "He's regular!"

Till now there was a supreme excitement of life Philip had never experienced, the Lindbergh welcome, the thrill of a ticker tape arrival in New York. The placards proclaimed, "Welcome, Liz and Phil!" and every siren in the harbor blew a salute as they crossed from Staten Island toward the alluring skyscrapers.

At the Battery they changed to bubble-topped cars, and the blinding snowfall of tape, torn-up telephone books, confetti and streamers began.

The bubble cars which the police had prescribed insulated them from the excitement to a degree, and the city made a mistake, I think, in keeping Elizabeth and Philip apart by arranging that they should ride in separate cars.

In the second car beside Mrs. Averell Harriman, the Governor's wife, Philip found the plastic top getting gradually obscured with paper but the personal welcome of the crowds had a wild, sustained and unmistakable excitement. At City Hall, as the gunsmoke from the salutes swirled across the scene, the whole city seemed to take up the cry, "Liz! Liz! Phil! Phil!"

They ate lunch that day with fifteen hundred people and dinner at the Waldorf-Astoria Hotel with four thousand. Between the two meals, the Queen addressed the United Nations Assembly.

After the United Nations, they were both whisked to the Empire State Building, and had the satisfaction of enjoying the view they had heard so much about. Then Elizabeth returned to the Waldorf to rest while Philip energetically went to visit the American Institute of Physics on East 45th Street.

Coming back, his car and escort got held up in the rush-hour traffic. "Let's walk," said Philip. The security men could hardly believe their ears. "Let's walk," he repeated. "It can't be far."

And walk they did, from Lexington Avenue along a block of 45th Street to Grand Central Station. They went briskly through the station onto Park Avenue and then passed through an underground garage to the side entrance of the Waldorf on 50th. They were not recognized anywhere. Photographs of Philip beamed from every shop window. His name flared in the headlines. Hundreds of people in the passing crowd must have waited on the sidewalks earlier in the day. At the hotel another crowd had gathered, awaiting his car. As Philip tried to push through, they said indignantly, "Stop shoving!"

"It's me," said Philip as he reached a policeman.

The policeman stared blankly. People in the crowd, awaiting the golden-haired man of their dreams, still didn't recognize him. The security men quickly got him through, of course. But it was one of those pieces of nonsense Philip loved, one of those dual-identity incidents that have always helped him keep his feet on the ground.

Chapter 17

◈ "The Most Governed Person"

1

LYING IN BED this morning, reflecting on this final chapter, I surprised myself with the realization that I have known Philip for nearly forty years. From time to time we have been icily distant cousins and at other times as close as twins in a carriage. We have often practiced an aloofness, as members of a family are apt to do—and then suddenly we get together.

"Cousins are foes and foes are friends," the old paradox goes. Looking back, I find another paradox, for I seem to have known a dozen Philips, all so astonishingly different that one almost imagines they are not the same person. Is the little boy rowing alone to the middle of the lake at Panka the selfsame Philip who stands on the saluting platform of the *Britannia* as it glides along the St. Lawrence Seaway?

His visits to Ghana and Italy are made; his 1959 tour of the Far East recedes in the memory; his second visit to the Yukon is accomplished. And I remember the slim young man who wistfully confided, "I should so like to see more—much more—of the world."

As I bring my cousin's biography up to the present, I have learned to doubt some of my conclusions about him or at least I find that early judgments can be faulty. I once thought Philip rather wrapped up in himself chiefly because he displayed a power of concentration and absorption far beyond mine.

I once thought of him as ambitious, though I realize now that I might, perhaps, have made a wiser interpretation of his strong direction and drive. He is a planner and he takes pride in his ability to light up a routine and give it fresh polish or meaning so that it becomes something quite new.

In the past, I laughed with Philip and quarreled with him; I have been buoyed by his humor and have sometimes smarted under his satire. I once, to get even, scorned him in indignation over a family matter that quite eludes me now. Probably every man has as many different selves, each within the others. Sometimes I read of a Philip of popular legend and can scarcely recognize the person I know.

At least one side of his character that is new to me was shown when, flying back from America, he and Elizabeth sentimentally celebrated the weekend of their tenth wedding anniversary at Broadlands. It was supposed to be a coincidence that they returned to the scene of their honeymoon then, but I know that Philip arranged things with Uncle Dickie. The occasion was an undoubted success, and in 1958 they went back again. As on each anniversary, Philip gave Elizabeth a huge box of white flowers.

Philip has a dreamy side, though he keeps it well hidden. I remember that he accomplished one of his more remarkable public performances when he attended a reunion of three thousand Wrens. He not only made the expected speech, "If you can do just a fraction in civilian life of what you did in the Navy . . ." but he then decided to tour the hall and mingle with them afterward, meeting many girls he remembered. My husband is inclined to think this a rarely excelled feat of *savoir-faire*, but the truth is that Philip is nostalgic about his old days and old friends in the service.

He used to be fond of attending naval reunions and similar stag dinners until, I think, he was dismayed to discover that he had become increasingly an honored guest instead of just one of the group.

A share of Elizabeth's loneliness on the throne has been forced on him by his sense of the dignity of the Crown. Although such activities as the polo club break through this isolation and he probably moves in a larger social set than has any leading member of the Royal House for generations, he is a dedicated figure, no less than his wife. But he pays a price for his loyalty.

2

The State visit to Holland in March 1958 had a friendly and festive air even to an interlude on the road between Utrecht and The Hague when Prince Bernhard of the Netherlands kidnaped Philip and they went roaring off for a trial spin in Bernhard's Ferrari sports car. Made at the time of the early tulip pageant, it was the first visit to the Netherlands in three centuries by a British sovereign. Certainly, it was the first meeting, during any State visit, of two such husbands.

The following month Philip traveled to Belgium to visit the British Pavilion at the Brussels World's Fair where, incidentally, he startled an exhibitor of bathroom fixtures with the question, "Why can't they make bathroom cisterns [tanks] less noisy?"

He visited Northumberland with the Queen but made a breathless dash afterward by royal barge, car, plane and car again to play polo at Windsor three hundred fifty miles south.

The already fast tempo of activities quickened still more. In November Philip paid a three-day flying visit to Canada to attend the world conference of the English-speaking Union.

One morning, Philip went on an early duck shoot, participated in the conference and still managed to reach the scene of a mining disaster in Springhill, Nova Scotia. A score of men had been entombed for more than eight days, and the disaster was a nightmare for Canada as well as for the stricken town. Philip talked to the survivors and one of the men, having endured the most harrowing experiences below ground, brightly asked him to autograph the plaster cast on his broken leg. He gladly obliged.

After this new quick-style Canadian junket, it was not surprising to find him returning over the Atlantic in a Comet IV in four hours and five minutes. The world had indeed shrunk for him. That same month, Philip visited his sister Theodora, in Germany.

"Are you keeping track?" a friend asked me, knowing that I was making a journal of Philip's many moves.

"It's almost a full-time job," I said and I quietly took from my desk a bulletin in French that had just come from the British Embassy. It announced that in 1959 he would travel another thirty-six thousand miles, visiting Pakistan, India and South East

Asia, and still the program failed to mention the royal journey to North America to open the Seaway, the visit to Ghana and many more projects that at that time still lay ahead.

3

"I have had very little experience of self-government. In fact I am one of the most governed people in the world." So said Philip in the middle of his Far East Tour of 1959. It was one of his many sayings that marry truth with wit, and this casual but important phrase endeared him immediately to his Asian hosts.

The tour, by Comet to Delhi, India, from Pakistan to Singapore, Sarawak, Borneo, Hong Kong, the Pacific Islands and the Bahamas, by the yacht *Britannia*, was timed to take him around the world in ninety-nine days.

Philip went first to India expressly to represent the British Association for the Advancement of Science at the Indian Science Congress, and to see something of the technological achievements of that vast country, as well as make acquaintance with the traditions of her past. It did not matter that, as so often happened now, a single visit blossomed—even in its planning stage—into a tour of considerable length and variety.

More important and to the point was the value of his personality in the Cold War of East and West. Marshal Nikolai Bulganin, Premier Khrushchev and others had all made the Asian Grand Tour with some persuasive success. Now it was Philip's turn, and from the moment when he stepped from the plane on a misty morning and said, "The last thing I expected was fog in Delhi!" events began going his way.

He was facing a tremendous challenge as well as responsibility.

In Bombay and other cities, India had only recently devoted a great deal of effort to tearing down the statues of British monarchs. Politicians, businessmen and university students had been showing vividly that they wanted nothing more of the pompous British and their stuffy ways. It was perhaps no more than Indian courtesy that girls at the airport began garlanding him until he could carry no more, but then he began garlanding them. "You keep it," he said to a sari-clad teenager offering another garland. "You keep it—and think of me!"

He had started off on the right foot. Receiving an honorary degree at Delhi University, he explained, "I regret to say my only degrees are honorary ones. This fact will become only too apparent during my address."

To the huge audience this was very different from the stiff and stern Raj of the past, and Philip continued to take them all with him by his easy gestures and graceful self-deprecations. It has been remarked that the success or failure of a royal tour is established with the press during the first three days. Philip established his new rapport within twenty-four hours.

Eleven years had passed since Uncle Dickie had ruled as the last Viceroy of India and flown home for Philip's wedding. Now, on India's Republic Day, Prince Philip rode beside Mr. Pandit Nehru, the Indian Premier, as a friend (as Earl Mountbatten had done), he was sleeping in Government House as his uncle had done, and the significance of the bond between the republic and the Monarchy did not need further underlining.

Philip went to the Himalayas to see the highest dam ever built in those rugged and turbulent gorges. He toured the atomic power plants of the new India and spent a day photographing the ancient temples carved in the volcanic rockface of Ajanta.

At the new capital of the Punjab region, he gazed at the Le Corbusier-designed blocks of apartments and listened carefully to the details of construction. Then he asked the question that had already been asked by the Indians themselves, "Yes, but are the people happy?" And this query caused a Punjabi newspaper to appear with the potent headline, "He is one of us!"

In Jaipur richly caparisoned elephants raised their trunks to greet him; in Madras, as the flowers piled up in his car, he delighted the crowds by tossing them back; and Calcutta, supposedly on the eve of Communist control, gave him the warmest welcome of all.

It was the same in Pakistan. The traffic in Karachi was stopped fifteen minutes before his car was due to pass and he apologized disarmingly for the disruption. His leading speech, delivered at the Pakistan Association for the Advancement of Science, broke away from stock phrases and pleaded for joint Commonwealth action on all scientific problems affecting industry and commerce. In a sack-making factory he found a novelty in royal greetings: hundreds of paper flags which the workers had fixed to their machines jigged up and down in a sea of color.

Philip had piloted the Comet himself when he landed at Karachi. En route from India, I should explain, he had made a detour over Katmandu that gave him one of the rare clear views of Everest and all its neighboring peaks.

After he visited the Khyber Pass on the famed northwest frontier, and was richly entertained by the Wali of Swat in his mountain capital, he flew on to Rangoon, Burma. Here, as it happened, a political crisis simmered among the palms and pagodas, and the Burmese orchestras scarcely sufficed to hide the commotion of armed guards that were flung around the royal visitor. But Philip was ashore for only thirteen hours.

His next concern was to rendezvous the *Britannia* with six ships of the Far East Fleet one hundred fifty miles from Singapore. As the royal yacht entered the Malacca Straits, the six vessels formed a three-column escort and a twenty-one-gun salute thundered in welcome.

In Singapore, even a Russian freighter did not fail to be flying colors in Philip's honor, though one doubts the Soviet skipper realized that he was greeting a grand-nephew of the Czar.

The pro-Communist mayor of Singapore had, in fact, called on the city to boycott Philip's arrival. But the Chinese New Year celebrations were in full swing and everyone was in carnival mood. A barrage of fire crackers greeted Philip in the streets, and university students added to the good humor by staging a mock welcome of their own.

A rival procession was arranged complete with an impostor duke in naval uniform. When the two parades collided, Philip, to the students' delight, stood up in his car and waved to his rival.

It has been said that the tour developed, in many aspects, into a rehearsal for future visits by Elizabeth, but in reality it stood alone. In Sarawak, for instance, Philip piloted his own plane from airstrip to airstrip to inspect oilfields and other developments in the jungle.

A report home gave a little of the local atmosphere in telling of a chieftain of the head-hunting Dyaks "lightly clad in a straw hat, a khaki jacket and a delicately tattoed bare backside," delivering a Royal Address in the Legislative Council.

At Jesselton, capital of North Borneo, were people who paddled downriver for three weeks to see the "Great Rajah" and Dusuns who trekked over the hills. They were seeing not only Philip but also such marvels as a water tap and electric light for the first time.

Buffalo races were held; a blowpipe and shield were presented and Philip read the lesson in the little local church. It all seemed one world, this grouping of Commonwealth countries and colonies to which the Prince had pledged himself.

In Hong Kong, encouraged by a small cheer, he climbed onto the back seat of the official car and started waving as he had done in India, Pakistan and Singapore, but the crowds eyed him curiously and stayed silent.

Then Philip remembered a Chinese girl, not ten years old, who used to work with the sampan women when he was with the destroyer *Whelp*. He had sometimes given her chocolate when she was with the others, chipping rust from the hull; he remembered her bright and rewarding smile. What had become of her? he asked many people.

The news of the hunt for Suzie Ho Kwai Ting spread through the city. She was found among the crowded junks and, in pretty silk pajamas, she was presented to Philip aboard the *Britannia*. From then onward Hong Kong greeted him with enormous enthusiasm, pleased that a prince had fully demonstrated the common touch. Comparatively sparse crowds had turned out on his arrival. Many, many thousands lined his farewell route.

The *Britannia* sailed for the Solomon Islands. On the mainland of Asia Philip left behind him bridges, dams and streets newly named Edinburgh.

Using his eyes and ears in the middle of the formalities he had learned a great deal of what was going on in the East, and would return home to communicate it.

Now his ship's course lay through heavy seas and tropical rainstorms. The royal yacht took action to avoid Hurricane Sally and then, with blue skies and calm seas replacing the storm, reached the Solomons precisely on schedule.

Far from normal shipping routes and irksome civilization, the *Britannia* was out of touch in the Pacific for days on end, sailing in remote and enchanted seas. I like to think of Philip in the Gilbert and Ellice Islands especially, enthroned in a flower-decked chair of state, which was borne aloft in triumph by hundreds of singing, swaying, grass-skirted women.

Visits to Christmas Island, Panama, the Bahamas and Bermuda were made in the last stages of the '59 round-the-world tour. In the ninety-nine days he had covered 19,700 miles by air and 16,300 miles in the *Britannia*.

"The Duke visits Britain!" announced one newspaper as he returned home but, by and large, more serious pundits praised his capacities and his energy. Commenting on his interests "not only in functions but also in world affairs, not only in populations but also in individuals," a leading editorial described him as epitomizing the best type of naval officer.

When he stepped from his airliner, after having greeted the Queen and Prince Charles while still aboard, he found cabinet ministers and many others waiting in a deputation of welcome.

Three days later he was at Windsor vigorously playing polo. A day or two more and he was driving his son back for the new term at school like any young father.

Yet by the end of 1959 he had traveled farther than any prince in the history of man, and soon he will not have left a single part of Queen Elizabeth II's territories unvisited.

As one reaches the present, the subject of a biography becomes a portrait that dissolves, so to speak, into the personality who will be in tomorrow's newspapers and in the solid records of history.

What will his next achievement be? What else can he attain? It is still not possible to assess my cousin Philip in rigid terms. The past speaks in its procession of events and character, but the future presents its constant—and ever-interesting—mystery.